# Street by Street

# YEOvIL

## CREWKERNE, SHERBORNE

**Barwick, Bradford Abbas, Ilchester, Marston Magna, Martock, Montacute, Poyntington, Sandford Orcas, Sparkford, Stoford, Stoke sub Hamdon, Thornford, Tintinhull, West Coker, Yeovilton, Yetminster**

GW01453125

**2nd edition January 2008**
© Automobile Association Developments Limited 2008

Original edition printed February 2003

Enabled by Ordnance Survey

This product includes map data licensed from Ordnance Survey® with the permission of the Controller of Her Majesty's Stationery Office. © Crown copyright 2008. All rights reserved. Licence number 100021153.

Published by AA Publishing (a trading name of Automobile Association Developments Limited, whose registered office is Fanum House, Basing View, Basingstoke, Hampshire RG21 4EA. Registered number 1878835).

Produced by the Mapping Services Department of The Automobile Association. (A03559)

A CIP Catalogue record for this book is available from the British Library.

Printed by Oriental Press in Dubai

Ref: ML139z

ii

National Grid references are shown on the map frame of each page.
Red figures denote the 100 km square and blue figures the 1 km square.
Example: page 3: Yeovil Bus Station 356 116

The reference can also be written using the National Grid two-letter prefix shown on this page, where 3 and 1 are replaced by ST to give ST5616.

## ST

Bramwell

Somerton

A372

Pitney

B3153

Wearne

Upton

B3151

Kingsdon

Langport

Long Sutton

A372

Heale

Curry Rivel

Knole

6

Willtown

Muchelney

12

A378

B3168

Ilch

Fivehead

Thorney

Long Load

Milton

Witcombe

A303

Isle Abbotts

Hambridge

Kingsbury Episcopi

Ash

20

21

22

Westport

Stembridge

Coat

Martock

Tintinhull

Chilthorne Dome

Puckington

Barrington

East Lambrook

A3088

30

31

32

HONITON

Stocklinch

South Petherton

A303

Stoke sub Hamdon

Montacute

Alvir

Whitelackington

Over Stratton

Seavington St Michael

Norton sub Hamdon

40

Odcombe

Ilminster

Lopen

Kingstone

Allowenshay

West Chinnock

East Chinnock

W C

Merriott

A30

Harding Moor

CHARD

A30

Hinton St George

Chillington

A356

Haselbury Plucknett

50

51

Hardington Marsh

Chaffcombe

Higher Chillington

A356

North Perrott

Purtington

Crewkerne

A3066

B3167

Cricket St Thomas

Hewish

B3165

Misterton

South Perrott

Whatley

Wayford

Clapton

## Scale of enlarged map pages 1:10,000  6.3 inches to 1 mile

EPTON MALLET

Galhampton
North Barrow
Babcary
South Barrow
Bratton Seymour
Wincanton
ANDOVER
B3081
A359
A371

**4**   **5**
North Cadbury
Sparkford
South Cadbury
A303
Woolston
Blackford   Maperton   Lattiford
North Cheriton
South Cheriton
A357
A303

**7 8**   Downhead
more
West Camel   Wales
Bridgehampton
**9**   **10**
Queen Camel
**11**
Sutton Montis
ilton
B3145
Charlton Horethorne
Abbas Combe
Templecombe
A357

**15**   **16**   **17**   **18**   **19**
Chilton Cantelo
Marston Magna
Rimpton
Corton Denham
Sandford Orcas
ton
Ashington
Milborne Wick
Yenston

**25**   **26**   **27**   **28**   **29**
West Mudford
Mudford
Adber
udford Sock
eovil
arsh
Up Mudford
Trent
B3148
Poyntington
Oborne
Milborne Port
A30
Purse Caundle

**35**   **36**   **37**   **38**   **39**
A359
Over Compton
Nether Compton
Stallen
Sherborne
Goathill
Stourton Caundle
**3**
Yeovil
A30

**43**   **44**   **45 46**   **47**
Barwick
Stoford
Bradford Abbas
Thornford
Longburton
North Wootton
A3030
Bishop's Caundle

**48**   **49**
Ryme Intrinseca
Beer Hackett
Yetminster
Lillington
Caundle Marsh
Holwell
King's Stag

Closworth
A37
Crouch Hill
Holnest

stock
Melbury Osmond
Leigh
Glanvilles Wootton
Pulham
B3146
B3143

DORCHESTER
Hermitage
Middlemarsh

**ST**

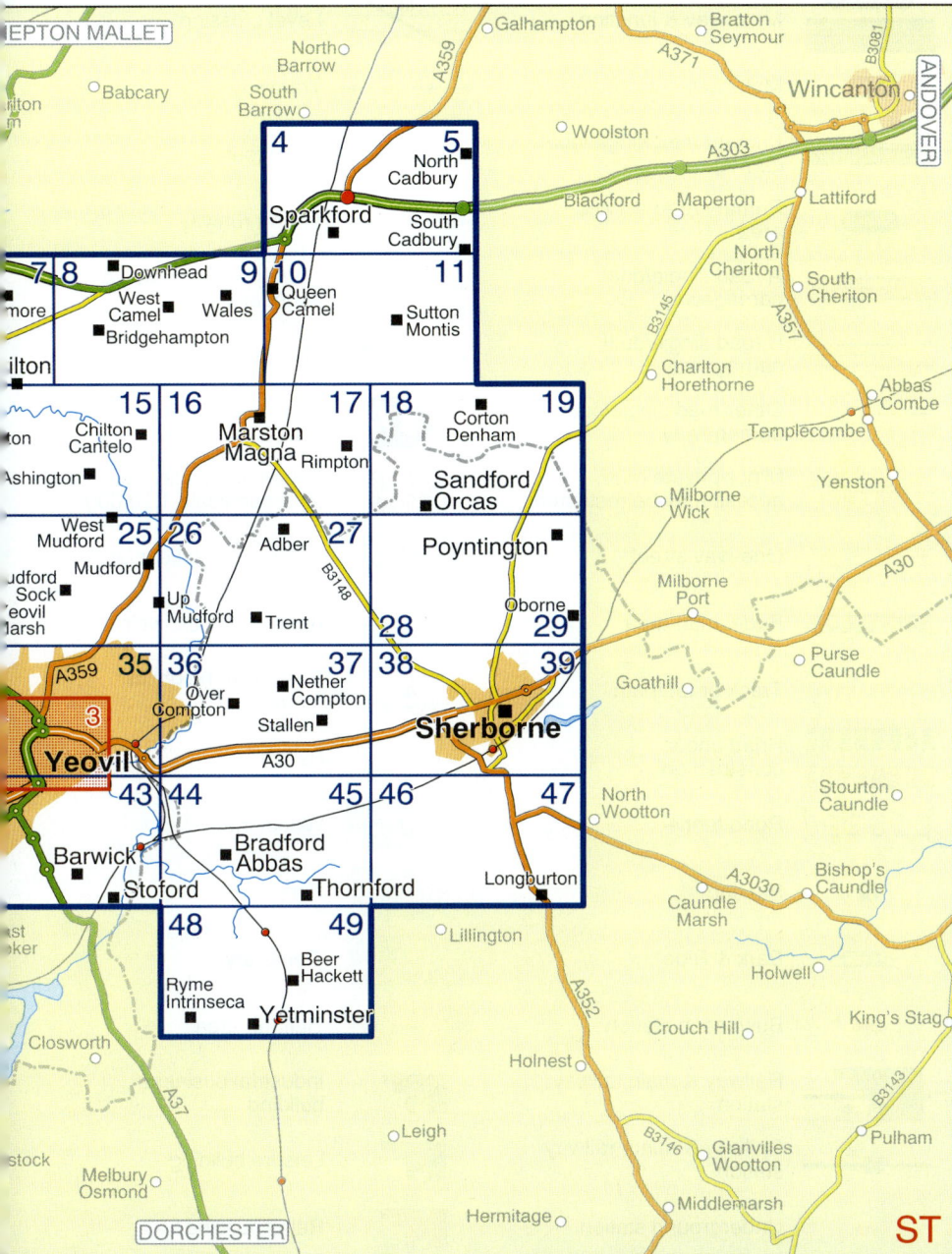

4.2 inches to 1 mile   **Scale of main map pages**   **1:15,000**

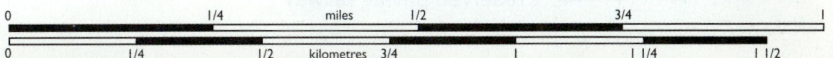

0   1/4   miles   1/2   3/4   1
0   1/4   1/2   kilometres   3/4   1   1 1/4   1 1/2

**iv**

| | |
|---|---|
| **Junction 9** | Motorway & junction |
| **Services** | Motorway service area |
| | Primary road single/dual carriageway |
| **Services** | Primary road service area |
| | A road single/dual carriageway |
| | B road single/dual carriageway |
| | Other road single/dual carriageway |
| | Minor/private road, access may be restricted |
| ← ← | One-way street |
| | Pedestrian area |
| -------------- | Track or footpath |
| | Road under construction |
| ⊢ - - - ⊣ | Road tunnel |
| **P** | Parking |
| **P+** | Park & Ride |
| | Bus/coach station |
| | Railway & main railway station |
| | Railway & minor railway station |
| ⊖ | Underground station |
| ⊖ | Light railway & station |
| +++++++++++ | Preserved private railway |

| | |
|---|---|
| *LC* | Level crossing |
| ●—●—●—● | Tramway |
| ----------- | Ferry route |
| ............... | Airport runway |
| — · — · — · — | County, administrative boundary |
| ⊲⊲⊲⊲⊲⊲⊲⊲⊲ | Mounds |
| ◀ **I7** | Page continuation 1:15,000 |
| ◀ **3** | Page continuation to enlarged scale 1:10,000 |
| | River/canal, lake, pier |
| | Aqueduct, lock, weir |
| 465 ▲ Winter Hill | Peak (with height in metres) |
| | Beach |
| | Woodland |
| | Park |
| | Cemetery |
| | Built-up area |
| | Industrial/business building |
| | Leisure building |
| | Retail building |
| | Other building |

| | | | | |
|---|---|---|---|---|
| City wall | | Castle | |
| A&E | Hospital with 24-hour A&E department | | Historic house or building |
| PO | Post Office | | Wakehurst Place (NT) | National Trust property |
| | Public library | | Museum or art gallery |
| i | Tourist Information Centre | | Roman antiquity |
| i | Seasonal Tourist Information Centre | | Ancient site, battlefield or monument |
| | Petrol station, 24 hour<br>Major suppliers only | | Industrial interest |
| † | Church/chapel | | Garden |
| | Public toilets | | Garden Centre<br>Garden Centre Association Member |
| | Toilet with disabled facilities | | Garden Centre<br>Wyevale Garden Centre |
| PH | Public house<br>AA recommended | | Arboretum |
| | Restaurant<br>AA inspected | | Farm or animal centre |
| Madeira Hotel | Hotel<br>AA inspected | | Zoological or wildlife collection |
| | Theatre or performing arts centre | | Bird collection |
| | Cinema | | Nature reserve |
| | Golf course | | Aquarium |
| ▲ | Camping<br>AA inspected | | Visitor or heritage centre |
| | Caravan site<br>AA inspected | | Country park |
| | Camping & caravan site<br>AA inspected | | Cave |
| | Theme park | | Windmill |
| | Abbey, cathedral or priory | | Distillery, brewery or vineyard |

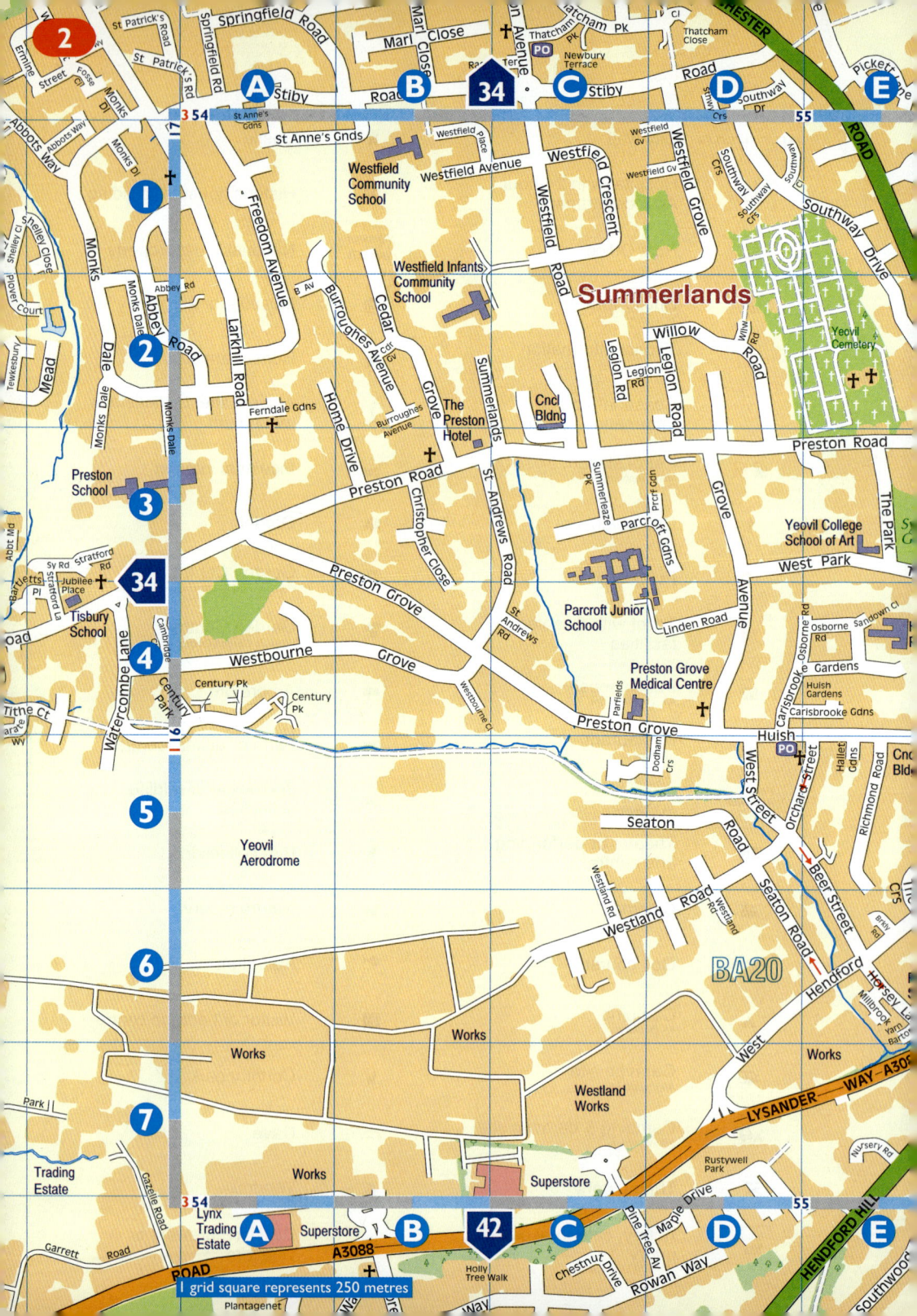

St Patrick's Road
Springfield Road
Mari Close
Thatcham Pk
Thatcham
Cl
RCHESTER

St Patrick's Rd
Springfield Rd
Newbury Terrace
Thatcham Close
Road
Pickett La

Fose
Di
St Patrick's Rd
PO

Ermine
Street

**A** Astiby
Road **B**
**34**
**C** Stiby
Road **D**
Southway
Dr
**E**

**3 5 4**
55

Monks Dr
Abbots Way
St Anne's
Gdns
St Anne's Gnds
Westfield Place
Westfield Gv
Westfield
Crs
Southway
Crs
Southway
Crs

**I**
Monks Di
Freedom Avenue
Westfield
Community
School
Westfield Avenue
Westfield
Westfield Gv
Westfield
Road
Westfield Grove

Shelley Cl
Shelley Close
Plover Court
Abbey Rd
Cedar Grove
Westfield Infants
Community
School
**Summerlands**
Willow
Winr
Rd
Yeovil
Cemetery

**2**
Monks
Dale
Abbey Road
Larkhill Road
B Av
Burroughes Avenue
Cdr
Gv
Legion Rd
Legion Rd
Legion Road
Southway Drive

Tewkesbury
Maen
Monks Dale
Ferndale Gdns
Burroughes
Avenue
Summerlands
Cncl
Bldg
Preston Road

**3**
Preston
School
Home Drive
The Preston
Hotel
Prcrft Gdn
Grove
The Park

Abbot Rd
Preston Road
Christopher Close
St Andrews Road
Summerleaze
Pk
Summerleaze
Parcroft Gdns
Yeovil College
School of Art
Sy
G

Sy Rd
Stratford Rd
Jubilee Place
Parcroft
West Park

Barwicks
Pl
Stratford La
**34**
Cambridge
Park
Preston Grove
St
Andrews
Rd
Parcroft Junior
School
Linden Road
Avenue
Carisbrooke Rd
Osborne Rd
Osborne Cl
Sandown Cl

Tisbury
School
Road
Westbourne
Grove
Grove
Preston Grove
Medical Centre
Carisbrooke Gardens
Huish
Gardens
Carisbrooke Gdns

**4**
Watercombe Lane
Century Pk
Century
Pk
Westbourne Ct
Parfields
Preston Grove
Huish
PO
Hallet
Gdns
Cncl
Bldg

Tithe Ct
ara e
Wy
Century Park
**9**
Dodham
Crs
West Street
Orchard Street
Richmond Road

**5**
Yeovil
Aerodrome
Seaton
Road

**6**
Westland Rd
Westland
Road
Westland
Rd
Seaton Street
Beer Street
Hornsey La

Works
Works
**BA20**
West
Hendford
Millbrook
Yard Barton

**7**
Cazelle Road
Works
Westland
Works
Works
Rustywell
Park
LYSANDER WAY-A30
Nursery La

Park
Superstore
Southw

Trading
Estate

**3 5 4**
55

**A**
Lynx
Trading
Estate
Superstore
**B**
**42**
**C**
Maple Drive
Rowan Way
**D**
Hendford Hill
**E**

Garrett
Road
ROAD
A3088
Holly
Tree Walk
Chestnut Drive
Pine Tree Av

Plantagenet

**1 grid square represents 250 metres**

# YEOVIL

**Grass Royal**

## Grid references (top)
F  G  H  35  J  K

## Grid references (right side)
I · 2 · 3 · 35 · 4 · 5 · 6 · 7

## Grid references (bottom)
F  G  H  43  J  K

## Labelled features and roads

MUDFORD ROAD
Folly F
St George's Av
St David's Crs
Avenue
Milford Park
Milford Rd
Wingate
Netherton
Charles Road
Mayfield Road
Rosebery
Percy
Alexandra Road
Cromwell Rd
St Michael's
Lingfield Av
Works
Glenville Rd
Sunningdale Rd
PO
Highfield Trading Estate
Hill Crest Rd
Hillcrest Cl
Melrose Road
Cheston Avenue
Milford Rd
Crest Road
St Michael's Avenue
Highfield Road
Fielding Rd
Surgery
Grass Royal Junior School
St Michael's Cl
St Avon Cl
College Green
Goldcroft
Kenmore Drive
Longcroft Rd
Portreeve Dr
Valley Clse
Fielding Road
North Ter
Gordon Road
Grass
Royal Cl
St Thomas Cross
Pen Mill Infant School
Sparrow Road
Roping Road
Mitchelmore Road
Kingston Vw
King Street
Crofton Avenue
Summerhouse Wy
Eastland Road
Mt Pleasant
Matthews Road
Works
Wyndham Vw
KINGSTON
Yeovil Bowls & Squash Club
The Park School
Higher Kingston
Yeovil District Hospital
A&E
St Gildas RC Primary School
Crofton
Goldcroft
Kiddles
Works
Westville
Eastville
Southville
Works
SHERBORNE ROAD
Gt Western Ter
Wyndham
Wyndham Hill
A37
A30
RECKLEFORD
Cattle Market
Fire Station
Reckleford Infant Sch
Hillside Ter
Hill Vw Ter
Job Centre
Superstore
The Park
Park Road
Court Ash
Mt Cecil Street
North Lane
Vincent Pl
Central Road
Ambulance Station
Earle
Dampier St
Ivel Court
Monarch's Way
Riverside Walk
Clarence St
Princes Street
Church street
Market St
PO
The Quedam Shopping Centre
Ivel Square
Central Rd
Works
Cineworld
Yeo Leisure Park
Westminster
Hendford
High St
Middle St
PO
Unicn
Yeovil Bus Station
Old Station Rd
S Western
The Manor Hotel
CAB
Mus of South Somerset
Cncl Bldg
Peter Street
Clinc
Bond St
Cncl South Bldg
Yeovil Coll
Stars Lane
Old Station
Hendford Grove
Surg
Penn Hill
Park St
Addlewell
Mll Lane
Works
Newton Road
Law Courts
St Nicholas Cl
St Nichl Cl
Summerhouse Ter
Mill Lane Trading Est
River
Penn House Day Hospital
Maltravers House Council & Govt Offices & Register-Office
Addiewell La
Monarch's Way
Ski Centre
Johnson Hall & Octagon Theatre
Penn Park
Penn Hill
Penn Hl Pk
Swan Theatre
Brunswick St
Park St
Aldondale Gdns
Goldenstones Pool & Leisure Centre
Nine Springs Park
Summerhouse Hill
Newton Surmaville

A · B · C · D

Parsonage Farm   3 60   Foster's Lane

**South Barrow**

Musmoor La

Chapel Lane

Nightingale Lane

Sparkford Road

1

Forty Acres Farm

2

27

Hazlegrove Preparatory School

Sparkford Wood

Haynes International Motor Museum

M

A359

3

Sparkford Road

A303

Brains Lane

The Avenue

**Sparkford**

PH

Long Hazel Park

High Street

Cherry Pie Lane

Cobb Flds

Orchard Close

Church Road

4

26

Twines Close

Ainstey

Dr

Green Close

Manor Close

Church Road

5

A303

A359

PO

Gason

A303

A · B · 10 · C · D

Sparkford Hill Lane

3 60

61

Sparkford Hill

28

1 grid square represents 500 metres

E
F
A359
G
**North Town**
Higher North Town Lane
Lower North Town Lane
H
Way

62
63
28

Cary Road

Cadbury Park Farm

Cadbury Business Park

The Close

**I**
Chapel La
**Brookha**

North Cadbury CE Prim Sch

Monarch's Way

Coxs Close

Curry La

Ridgeway

Lane

Cary Road

High Street

PO
**2**
Wo

**North Cadbury**

27

North Cadbury Cou

side

River Cam

Parish Hill

Monarch's Way

**3**

A303

*Chapel Cross*

**4**

26

Chapel Road

**Little Weston**

**South Cadbury**

Folly Lane

Folly Lane

Compton Road

**5**

62
63

E
F
Leland Trail
**II**
G
Castle Lane
H
**Ea En**

side

**6**

**Kingsdon**

Special School

A  3 52  B  C  53  D

Brincil Hill

B3151

**1**

25

Red Post Cross

EDMOND'S HILL

Park Brook

A372

er Road

**2**

BONDIP HILL B3151

A303

**3**

24

South
Mead Farm

Blackthorne
Close

Little
Meadow

**4**

Ilchester Community
School (Junior)

Taranto
Hill

Channel
Dash
Pl

Ilstrs Crs

Hermes Pl

Ilchester
Community
School
(Infant)

Eagle Cl

Briarfield  Millfield

Dragonfly Close

Esmonde Dr

Central Av

B3151

Gn

Costello Ditch

COSTELLO  HILL  B3151

Bir

**5**

23

A303

Great
Orch

Great
Orch

Orch

**Northover**

A  3 52  B  **13**  C  53  D

Lane

Works

Priory Cl

**Ilchester**

Leland Trail & Monarch's Way

1 grid square represents 500 metres

Town
Hall

PO

MAR

Back La

Ivel Gdns

PH

Pill Brie

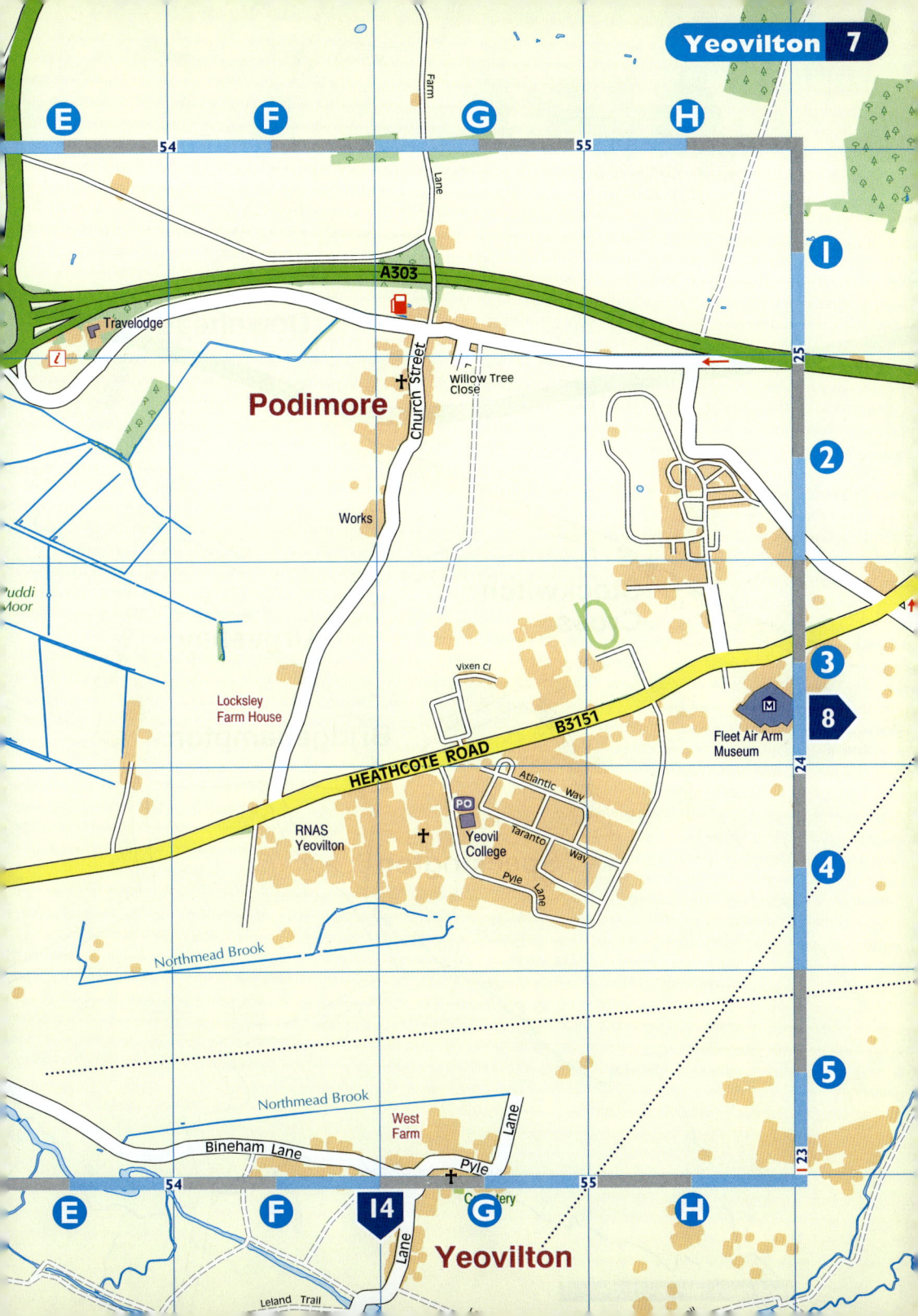

E F G H

54 55

**I**

A303

Travelodge

Farm Lane

**Podimore**

Church Street

Willow Tree Close

25

**2**

Works

Puddi Moor

Vixen Cl

**3**

Locksley Farm House

Fleet Air Arm Museum

**8**

HEATHCOTE ROAD    B3151

Atlantic Way

PO

RNAS Yeovilton

Yeovil College

Taranto Way

Pyle Lane

24

**4**

Northmead Brook

**5**

Northmead Brook

West Farm

Pyle Lane

Bineham Lane

23

54 55

E F G H

**14**

Cemetery

Lane

**Yeovilton**

Leland Trail

A   B   C   D

3 56    57    Slate Lane

Annis Hill

Lane   Track

1

25

**Downhead**

A303

Plowage Lane

Keep St

2

Slow Ct La

Leland Trail

B3151

**Stockwitch Cross**

3

**Urgashay**

Chantry Lane

Leland Trail

7

Fleet Museum

24

Speckington Lane

**Bridgehampton**

4

**Speckington**

Leland Trail

5

1 23

Hornsey Brook

3 56    57

A    B    15    C    D

I grid square represents 500 metres

E  F  G  H

58  59

Gason

I

Parson's
Steeple

Canegore
Corner

Howell
Hill

Traits
Lane

Wales

Blackwell Road

Countess Gytha
Primary School

Laurel
La

Leland Trail

Englands Lane

Englands Md

Green
La

Works

Mildmay Dr
Orchard
Ct

Mildmay Dr

The Walnut
Tree Hotel
PH

River Cam

Church Path

Church Pth

The Glebe

Surg
PO

Queen C
Health C

elza
t
Street

Back
Street

Leland Trail

Church Pth

Wales
Lane

Queen
Camel

The Glebe

Cleaveside Cl

Rectory Farm

Old Farm Close

West Camel
Farm

Parsonage Road

West
Camel

West Camel Road

West Camel Road

STREET

A359

**2**

**3** Camel
Farm

**10**

24

**4**

Spring
Farm

Lambrook
Farm

CAMEL STREET

**5**

23

58  59

E  F  **16**  G  H

Little

Woollen Lane

A359

**Marston**

**10**

Gason

A359

PO

**A**      3 60     **B**      4      **C**     61      **D**

Church Road

†

Sparkford Hill Lane

**1**

Sparkford Hill

*River Cam*

Lane

Countess Gytha
Primary School

Rectory
Lane

†

25

Laurel La

Church

†

Grace Martin's La

**Westo**
**Bampf**

Englands Md

Englands Lane

Green
La

Works

Mildmay Dr

**2**

The Glebe

PO

Surg

Mildmay
Dr

Orchard Pl

A359

HIGH STREET

**ueen**
**amel**

Cleaveside Cl

Rectory Farm

Old Farm Cc

Queen Camel
Health Cen

Leland Trail

Leland Trail

Road

Road

**3**

Camel
Farm

Bindwell Lane

**9**

24

Windsor
Farm

**4**

Lambrook
Farm

STREET

CAMEL

**5**

1 23

Woollen Lane

A359

**A**      3 60     **B**      17      **C**     61      **D**

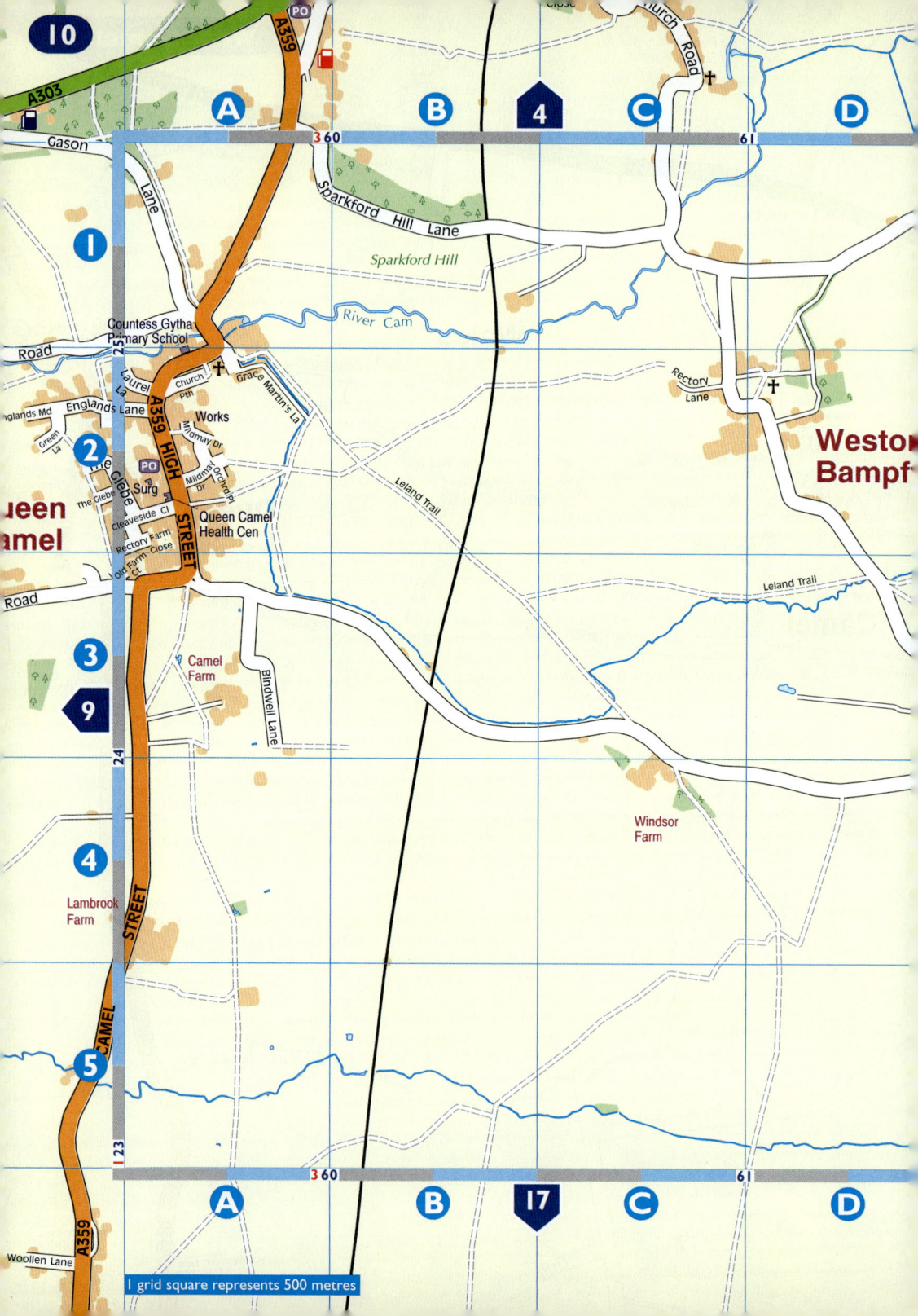

**1 grid square represents 500 metres**

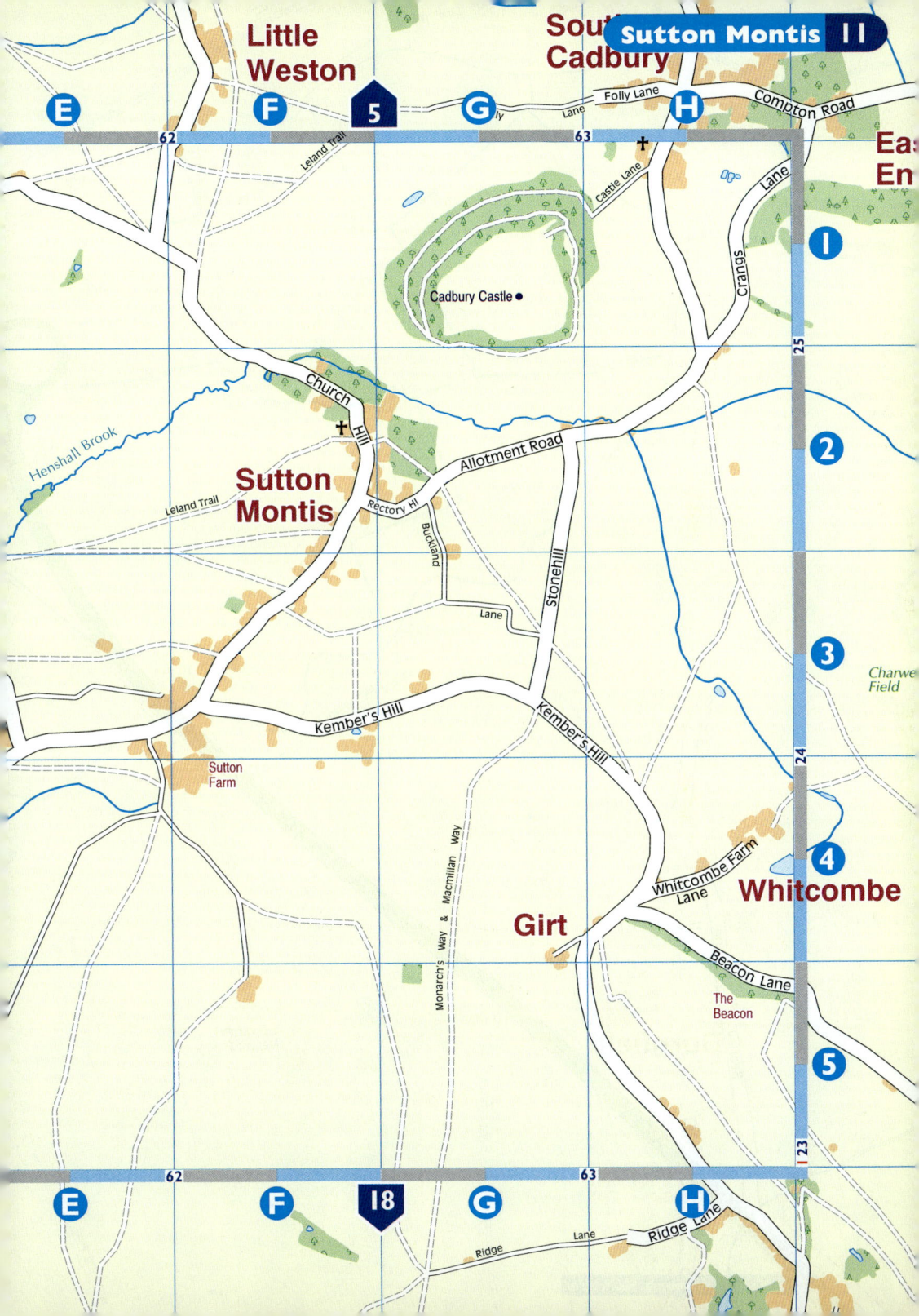

Little
Weston

South
Cadbury

Eas
En

Castle Lane

Crangs Lane

I

25

Cadbury Castle

Church Hill

Henshall Brook

Leland Trail

Sutton
Montis

Rectory Hl

Allotment Road

Buckland

Lane

Stonehill

2

3

Charwe
Field

24

Kember's Hill

Kember's Hill

Sutton
Farm

Monarch's Way & Macmillan Way

Whitcombe Farm Lane

Whitcombe

4

Girt

Beacon Lane

The
Beacon

5

I 23

Ridge   Lane

**12**

A  B  C  D

3 50

51

River Yeo (Ivel)

Pill Bridge Lane

Bridge Lane (Track)

Bearley

**1**

Bearley Farm

**2**

**3**

Burlingham's Farm

Burlingham's Lane

A303

**4**

Bearley Lane

**5**

Broadleaze Farm

**Durnfield**

A303

Stonecroft Manor Farm

Monarch's Way

OAKLAND ROAD

A  B  **22**  C  D

3 50

51

1 grid square represents 500 metres

Little

E   F   G   H

**Northover**

6

52    53    23

B3151

Priory Cl

**Ilchester**

Ivel Gdns

Leland Trail & Monarch's Way

Works

Abbotts Road

Cnns

Ga

PO

Back La

I

Frrs Cl

Town Hall

Bshps

High St

PH

Priory Road

Wk

Surg   Kingshams

Pill Bridge Lane

Pill Bridge Lane

Almsha La

Freed

Manor Cans

Market Place

West Street

The Paddocks

**Limington Road**

Church St

Mill Lane

A37

Lyster Cl

Almshouse Lane

Cemetery

Movey Lane

Duck

2

22

**Ilchester Mead**

Leland Trail & Monarch's Way

Bearley Brook

A37

Elborough Lane (Track)

3

14

4

Elborough Lane (Track)

Oakley Brook

Higher Oakley Farm

21

's Way

5

BA22

52    53

E   F   G   H

23

Rushley Farm

Oak Far

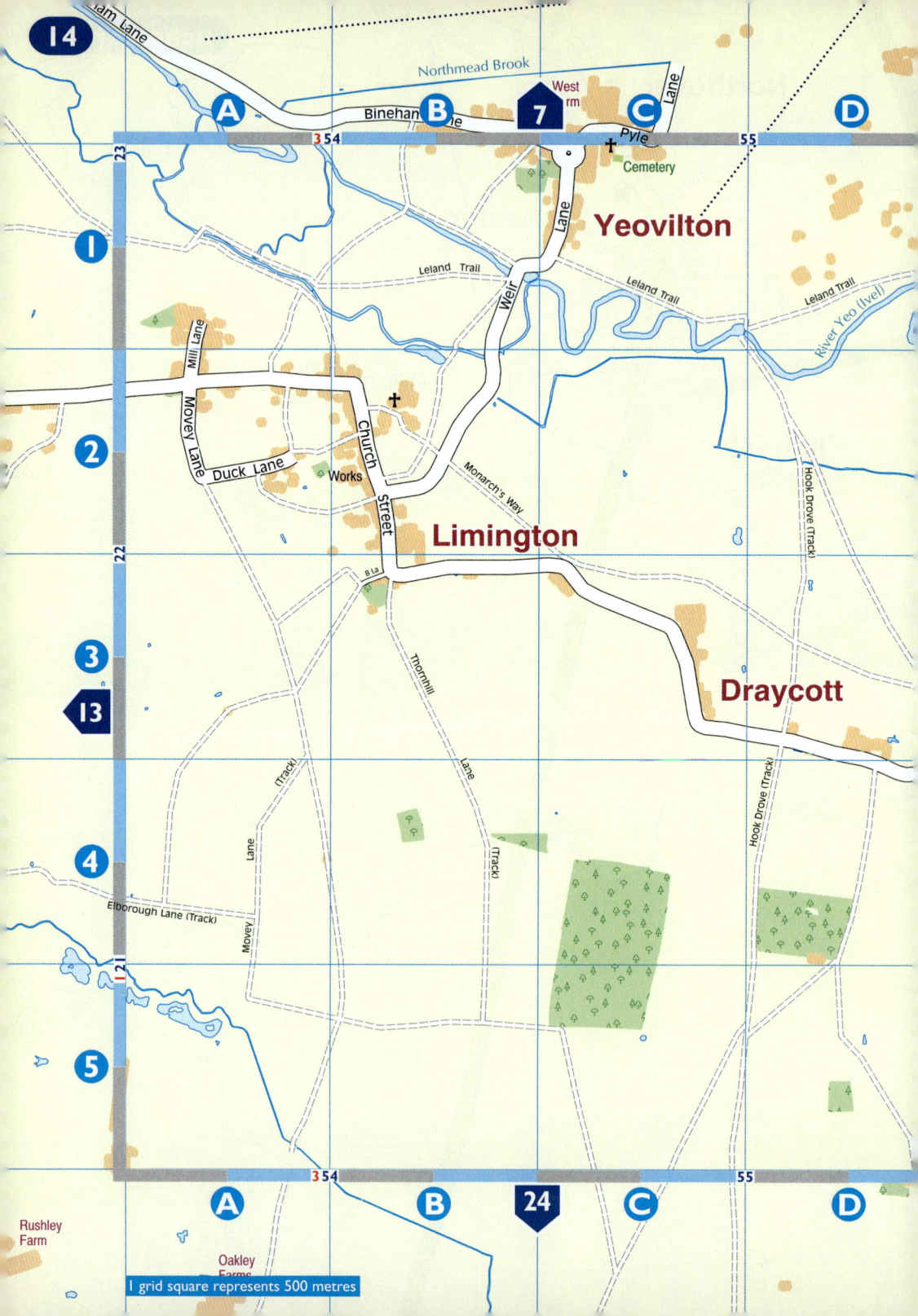

A  B  C  D

**23**

**354** **55**

I

Northmead Brook

Binehan Lane

West rm

**7**

Pyle Lane

Cemetery

**Yeovilton**

Leland Trail

Weir Lane

Leland Trail

Leland Trail

River Yeo (Ivel)

2

Mill Lane

Movey Lane

Duck Lane

Works

Church Street

Monarch's Way

**Limington**

B La

**22**

3

**13**

Thornhill

Lane

(Track)

**Draycott**

Hook Drove (Track)

Hook Drove (Track)

Lane

(Track)

4

Elborough Lane (Track)

Movey

Lane

**121**

5

Rushley
Farm

A  B  **24**  C  D

**354** **55**

Oakley
Farms

I grid square represents 500 metres

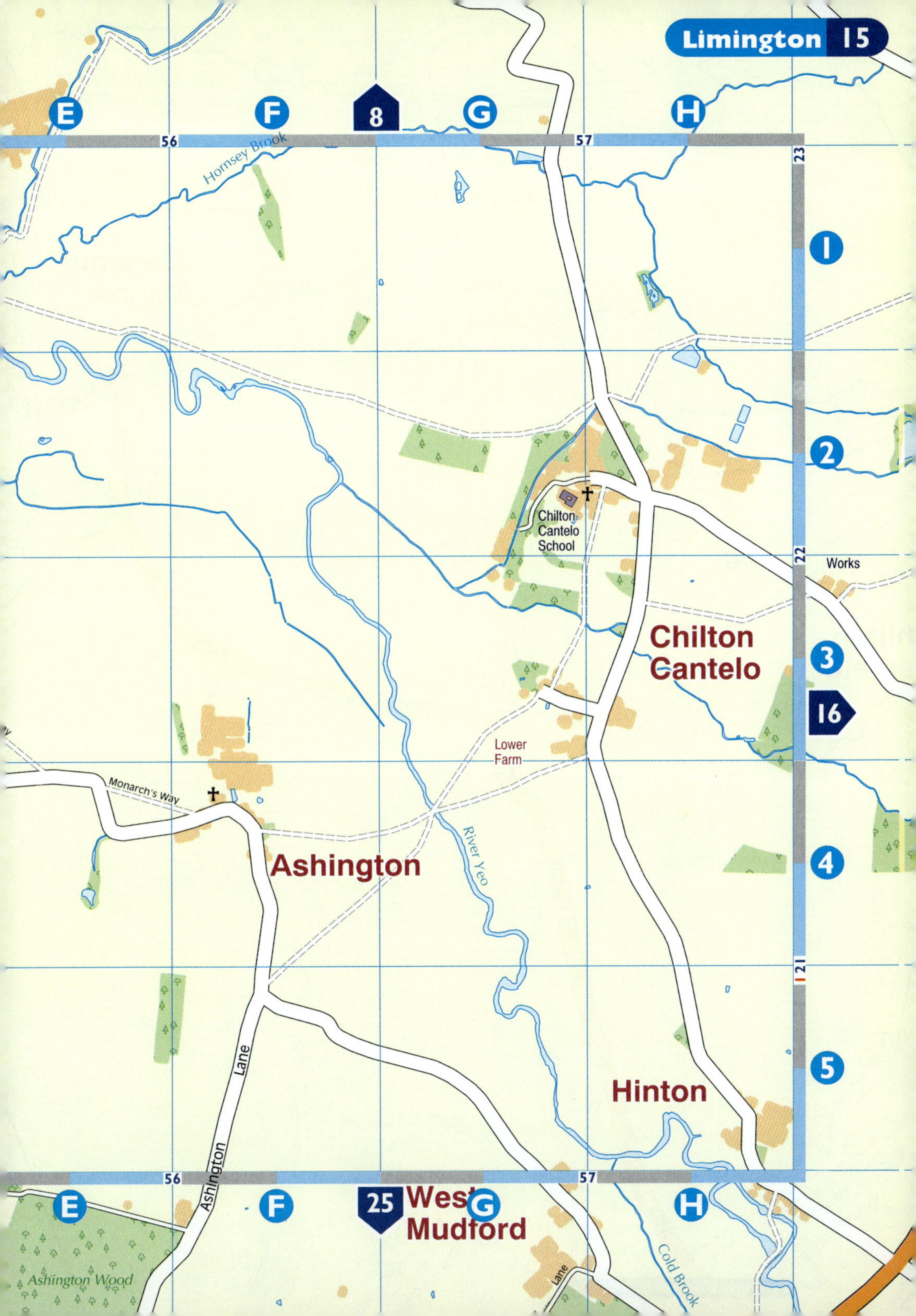

E

F

**8**

G

H

56

Hornsey Brook

57

23

I

2

22

Works

Chilton
Cantelo
School

**Chilton
Cantelo**

3

16

Lower
Farm

Monarch's Way

**Ashington**

River Yeo

4

21

5

**Hinton**

56

Ashington Lane

F

**25**

**West
Mudford**

G

57

H

E

Ashington Wood

Cold Brook

Lane

**16**

A    **3 58**    B    **9**    C    **59**    D

**1**

**23**

Little Marston Farm

Mill Stream

Little Marston Road

Woollen Lane

**Marston Magna**

Townsend

LTL MARSTON RD

**2**

A359

Church Wk

Garston Lar

Fiddle La

**22**

Works

Portway Farm

**3**

hilton antel

A359

**15**

Two Elms

Thorny Lane

**4**

A359

**21**

Thorny Lane

**5**

A    **3 58**    B    **26**    C    **59**    D

A359

Somerset Count
Dorset Cou

Brook

1 grid square represents 500 metres

E F **10** G H

60 61 **23**

**1**

Road
imperton Works Netherton Lane

Woodhouse Lane Woodhouse Lane

**2**

22

**3**

Mill Street

Home Farm Lane Middle Street

Back Lane Church Lane

High Street **18**

**Rimpton**

Roe Lane

Roe Lane

**4**

**Heaven's Door**

21

**Parkway**

B3148

RIMPTON HILL · B3148

Pitfield Corner

White Post

Slade Lane

Great Pit Lane

**5**

60 61

E F **27** G H

dber Great Pit Lane anmore Road Field Lane

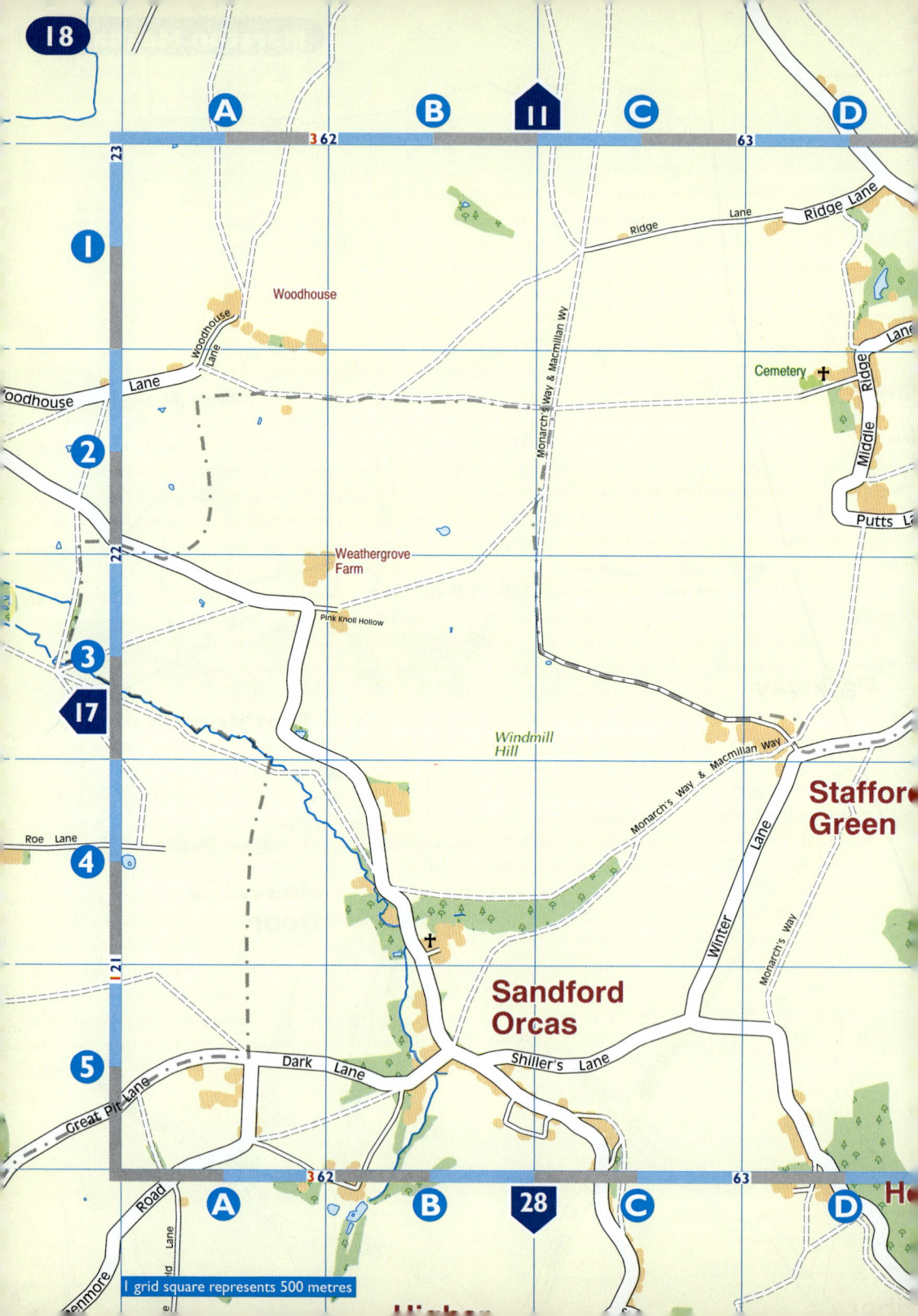

**A** 362 **B** **11** **C** 63 **D**

23

**1**

Woodhouse

Ridge Lane Ridge Lane

Woodhouse Lane

Woodhouse Lane

Monarch's Way & Macmillan Wy

Cemetery ✝

Middle Ridge Lane

**2**

22

Weathergrove Farm

Pink Knoll Hollow

Putts La

**3**

**17**

Windmill Hill

Monarch's Way & Macmillian Way

**Staffor Green**

Roe Lane

**4**

Winter Lane

Monarch's Way

21

**5**

✝

**Sandford Orcas**

Dark Lane

Shiller's Lane

Great Pit Lane

Road

362 **B** **28** **C** 63 **D**

**A**

enmore Lane

**He**

**E** Beacon 64 **F** **G** 65 **H** 23

**I**

Cowpath Lane

Down Farm

Charlton Field Lane

**Corton Denham**

Monarch's Way

Monarch's Way

**2**

B3145 22

Somerset County
Dorset County

Milborne Down

**3**

River Yeo

**4**

21

Poyntington Down

**5**

**E** 64 **F** 145 **29** **G** 65 **H**

**Poyntington**

**20**

Coat

Stapleton

Highway

Ash CE Primary Sch

Main

Cemetery

**A**  **B**  **C**  **D**

3 46 Business Park

Street

Coat Road

Lavers Oak

Stapleton

Oakland Dr

Oakland Rd

Great Western Road

Stapleton Road

B3165

Martock Business Park

Close

Bracey Road

Martock Lane

The Horses Shoe

Lyndhurst Dv

Snhrst

Works Business Centre

Wheelers

Win Close

Mar

Steppes Meadow

**1**

TA12

**Martock**

The Acres

Limbury

Old Market

Hills Orchard

Palfield

Mowl Barton

Printers Ct

North Street

B3165

Wst Cl

**2**

Hill Brook

Hills Farm

Hills Orch

Hill's La

Birch Rd

Steppes Crs

Cl

Paulls

Works

Rope Wk

Bearley Bridge Rd

Br Rl

Vincent

Wy

Moorlands Cl

Foldhill Lane

Foldhill Lane

Chestnut Rd

Beech Road

Elmleigh Rd

Myrtle Rd

Ashfield Park

Moorlands Pk

Little Orch

Bearley Road

Foldhill

Lndn Sq

Eastfield

**3**

ads Brook

Hinton Meads

Lane (Track)

19

Martock CE Prim Sch

Church Cl

Surg

Moorlands Pk Shop Cen

PO

East Street

East Street Drove

PH

Pound Lane

Church Street

Treasurer's House (NT)

Hurst Brook

Madey Mill Stream

Water Street

Stoke Road

**4**

Parrett Trail

Marturlong Cl

B3165

Hurst

Hurst Park

**Hurst**

Stoke Road

River Parrett Trail

**Bower Hinton**

River Parrett

Highfield Ter

PO

Hollies Cl

River Parrett Trail

North Street

River Parrett Trail

Kings Rd

**5**

Broad Wk

Broad Wy

Blind Lane

Bower Hinton

The Hollies Hotel

Middle St

Watcombe Cl

W Cl

aston's ne

Back Lane

Barton Cl

Higher St

3 46

**A**  **B**  **30**  **C**  **West Stoke**  **D**

River Parrett Tr

Ringwell Hill

A303

Works

Becks Rd

Tiptoft

Glovers Cl

1 grid square represents 500 metres

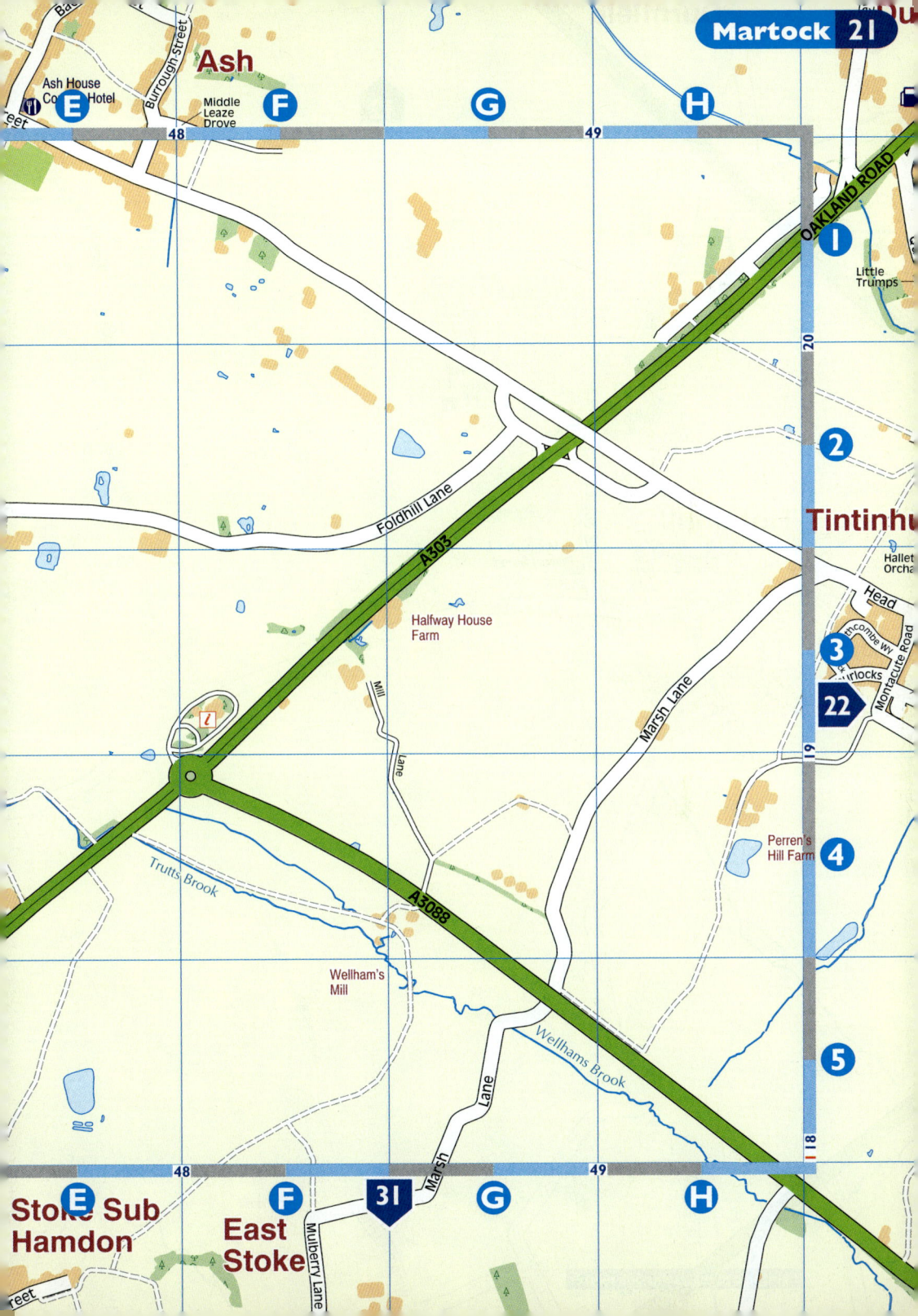

**Ash**

Ash House
Co... Hotel

(E)

Middle
Leaze
Drove

(F)

(G)

(H)

OAKLAND ROAD

(1)

Little
Trumps

20

(2)

**Tintinhu**

Hallet
Orcha...

Head

(3)

Montacure Road

**22**

...combe W...

...rlocks

19

Foldhill Lane

A303

Halfway House
Farm

Mill
Lane

Marsh Lane

Perren's
Hill Farm

(4)

Trutts Brook

A3088

Wellham's
Mill

Wellhams Brook

(5)

18

**Stoke Sub
Hamdon**

(E)

(F)

**31**

Marsh
Lane

(G)

(H)

**East
Stoke**

Mulberry Lane

48

49

48

49

# Durnfield

Manor Farm

Bearle

A303

OAKLAND ROAD

A B **12** C D

3 50 51

I

20

Little Trumps

Queen Street

Willey La

Tintinhull House (NT)

Church St

Farm Street

2

# Tintinhull

Vicarage Street

St Margarets CE Primary School

School Cl

Hallets Orchard

St Margaret's Road

Sock Farm

Head Street

Yeovil Road

Monarch's Way

Way

Monarch's

3

**21**

19

Southcombe Wy

Thurlocks

Montacute Road

Montacute Road

Cole Cross

Perren's Farm

4

Monarch's Way

5

I 18

3 50 51

A B **32** C D

Windmill Lane

Windmill Farm

's Water

E    F    13    G    **BA2**H

I

Oak
Farm

Rushley
Farm

2

Shortland
Farm

A37

Oakley        Lane

Halfway Caravan
& Camping Park

3

ILCHESTER ROAD

24

Kings Hill

Vagg
Lane

Lane

Vagg

4

**Chilthorne
Domer**

Forts
Orchard

Street

Main

Sammons

Little

Lane

Vagg

5

Axesclose Farm

Chilthorne
Domer Church
School

Tintinhull Road

Vagg Farm

Tintinhull Roa

Larkhill

Road

E    F    33    G    H

**Thorne
Coffin**

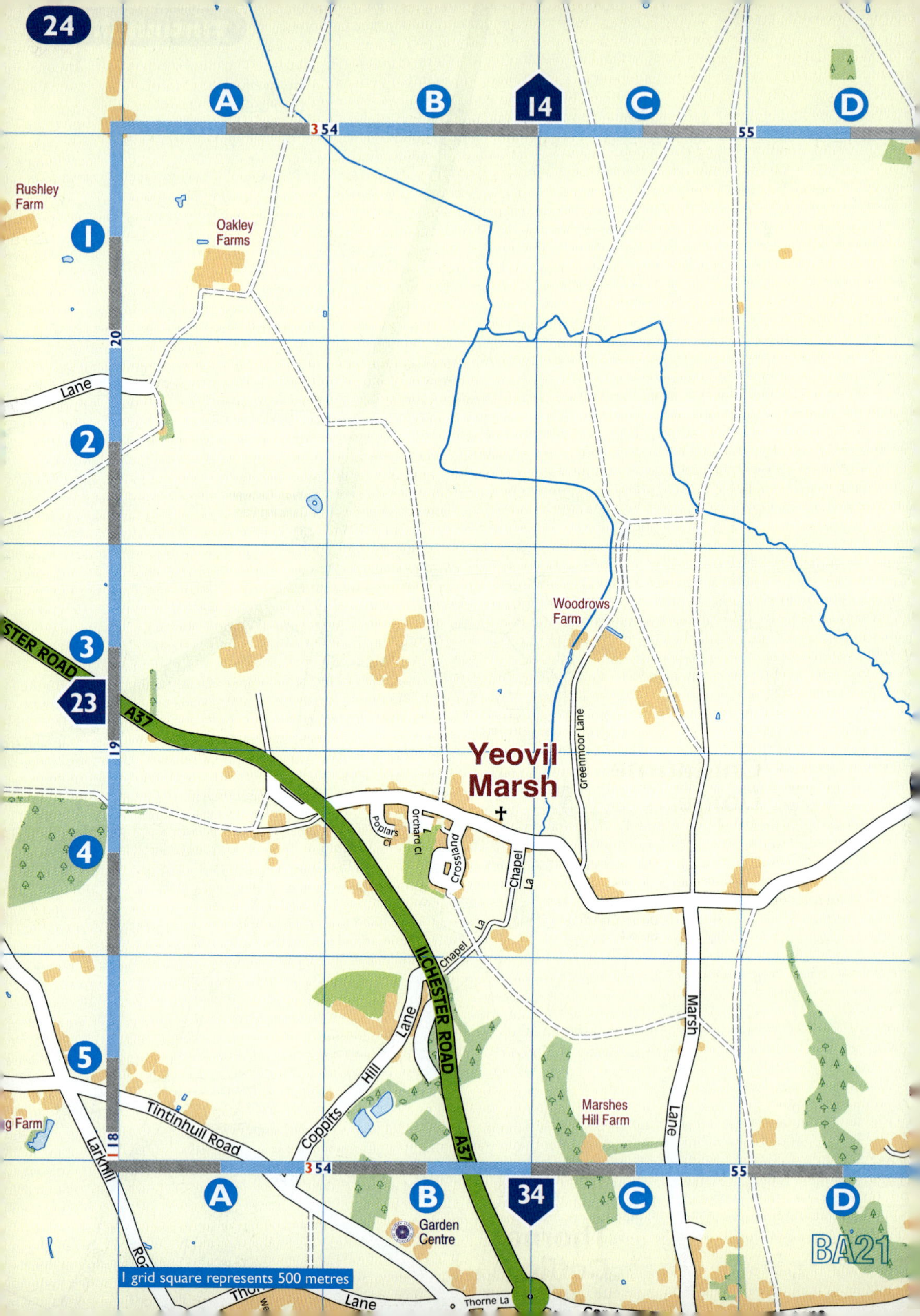

24

A  B  14  C  D

3 54  55

Rushley Farm

1

Oakley Farms

20

Lane

2

STER ROAD

3

23

A37

19

4

Woodrows Farm

Greenmoor Lane

Yeovil Marsh

Poplars Cl

Orchard Cl

Crossways

Chapel La

Chapel La

5

18

Larkhill

Tintinhull Road

ILCHESTER ROAD

Hill Lane

Coppits

A37

Marshes Hill Farm

Marsh Lane

g Farm

A  B  34  C  D

3 54  55

Garden Centre

BA21

Thorne La

Lane

**Hinton**

E F **15** G H

**I**

**West Mudford**

Cold Brook

**Mudford**

Deacons La PO

**2**

Ashington Lane

Ashington Wood

Woodside Farm

Monarch's Way

Droveway Lane

Hayes Meadow

**Mudford Sock**

A359

Sock Lane

Cold Brook

Monarch's Way

Sock Lane

**3**

Cemetery

**26**

Sockhill Farm

**4** Primrose La

**Up Mu**

Stone Farm

Primrose Lane

**5**

Lane

MUDFORD HILL

Primrose Lane

Lyde Road

E **35** F G H

A359

Hundred Stone

Fairmead Special School

Tower Road

Runnymede Road

Constable Cl

Redwood Road

**ROAD**

A  B  **16**  C  D

3 58  59

I

20

A359

**2**

Deacons La

PO

Somerset County
Dorset County

Monarch's Way

Hummer
Farm

Thorny Lane

Hales Meadow

A359

**3**

Cemetery

**25**

19

Manor
Farm

Primrose La

**4**

Primrose Lane

**Up Mudford**

River Yeo

Monarch's Way

Gor

Bir

Monarch's Way

Fisher's Cl

Youngs
Endowed
Primary School

Church
Farm

PH

**5**

Dorset County
Somerset County

Mill Lane

18

Trent Brook

Trent Cl

Redwood Road

Sandiewood

3 58  59

A  B  **36**  C  D

E   F   G   H

RIMPTON

Pitfield Corner

Lane

Great Pit Lane

White Post

17

60

61

B3148 HILL

I

Great Pit Lane

Road

Middle ... Lane

dber

Rowbarrow Hill

Rowbarrow Hill

Penmore

Moor

Penmore Road

20

2

Birch Hill

B3148

3

28

19

Ham Lane

Rigg Lane

Malthouse Lane

Ham Lane

Patson Hill Lane

4

Trent Barrow

nt

Lane

Plot Lane

Down Lane

Monarch's Way

Co

B371

5

Monarch's Way

18

60

61

E   F   37   G   H

**28**

Great Pit Lane

Dark Lane

Shiller's Lane

**A**

**B**

**18**

**C**

**D**

3 62

63

Ho

Road

**I**

Penmore

20

Middle Field Lane

Higher
Sandford

Spring Lane

Macmillan Way

Moorway Lane

Moorway Lane

**2**

Sandford Orcas Road

**3**

Monarch's Way

Golf C

Sherborne
Golf Club

**27**

19

H
F

Patson Hill Lane

Clatcombe Lane

Ambrose
Hill

**4**

**5**

Coombe Lane

Coombe
Farm

Macmillan Way

B3148

Monarch's Way

Sandford Orcas Road

118

3 62

63

**A**

**B**

**38**

**C**

Sandford Orcas Road

**D**

MARSTON

1 grid square represents 500 metres

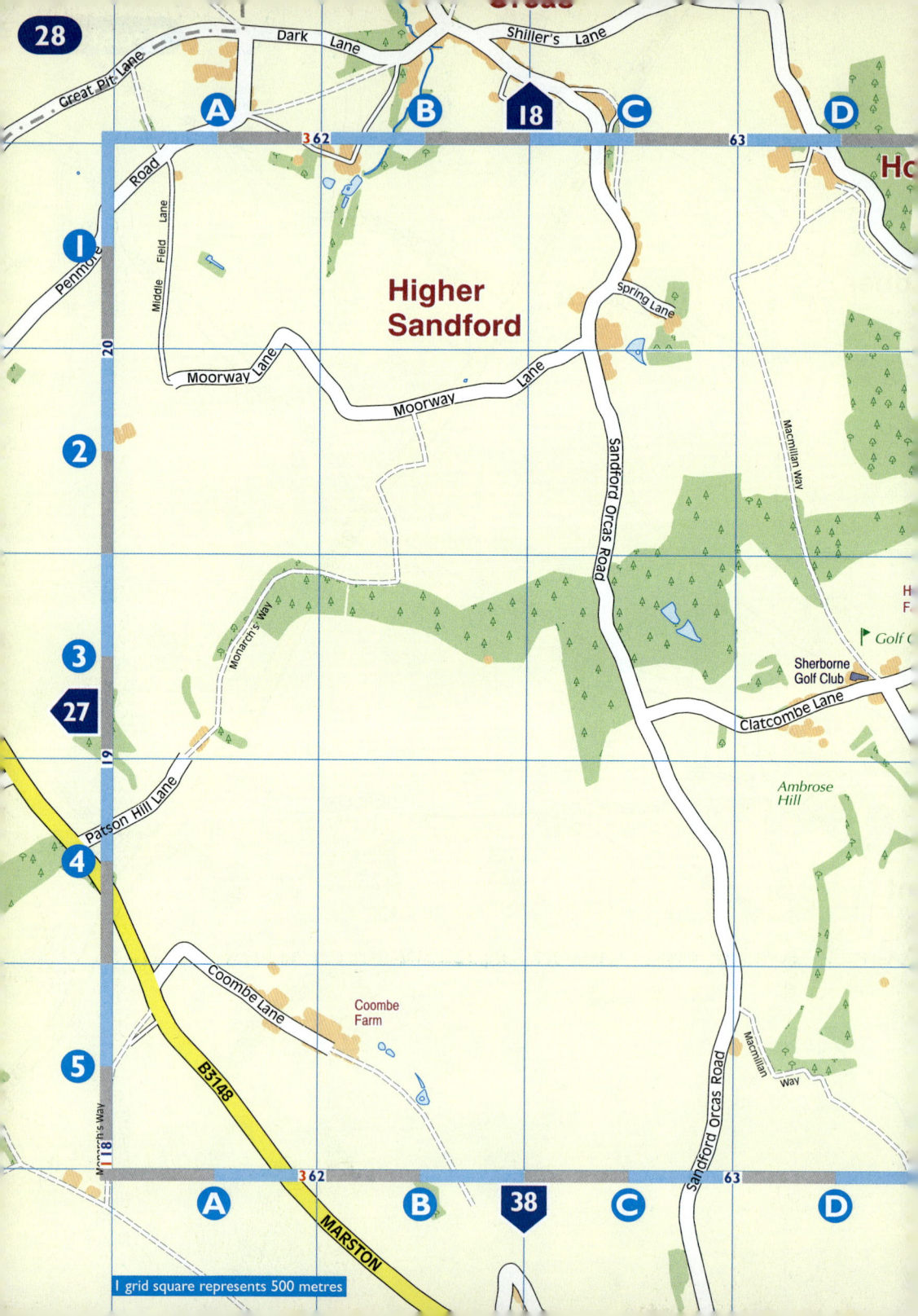

E  64  F  **19**  G  65  H

**Poyntington**  **I**

Red
Post

The Ridge

**20**

**2**

Clatcombe Lane

B3145

**3**

Lower Boyston Lane

**19**

**4**

The Grange
Hotel

**Oborne**

**5**

Castle Town Way

**18**

E  64  F  **39**  G  65  H

The Gryphon
School

CRACKMORE

ROAD B3145

St Aldhelm's Road

Castle

Coldharbour
Business Park

A30

Blackmarsh
Farm

Gaston's Lane

Broad Way

Broad Wy

Highfield Ter

PO

Hollies Cl

BOWER HINTON

Blind Lane

Middle St

Black Lane

81

Barton Cl

Higher St

B3165

**A** 3 46 **B** **20** **C** 47 **D**

River Parrett Trail

The Hollies Hotel

Works

Ringwell Hill

Cripple Hill

RINGWELL HILL

**1**

A303

River Parrett Trail

Works

**West Stoke**

North

Woodcombe Cl

Wd Cl

Rd

Succ

Glovers Cl

Great Field Lane

Tiptort

Becks Fld

cole La

Brocks Mt

Landlands

Hamdon Hill VW

Works

Stoke Sub Hamdon Priory

The Avenue

Hamdon Cl

Matt's La

West Street

Works

Hamdon Medical

Small Moor Brook

117

**2**

A303

PROPHET'S LANE

West Street

Norton Road

TA14

Petherton Bridge

River Parrett

**3**

A356

**Norton Sub Ha**

Norton Sub- Hamdon CE Primary School

**4**

New Road

Hamdon Vw

Barn Orch

Great Street

Works

Church La

Glebelands

Broadmea

Skinner's La

916

**5**

Higher Street

PO

Little Street

Minchington's Close

Little Mead

River Parrett Trail

Barrows Lane

River Parrett Trail

**A** 3 46 **B** 47 **C** **D**

A356

Manor Farm

**E**    **F**    **21**    **G**    **H**

48    49    18

**Stoke Sub Hamdon**

**East Stoke**

Marsh Lane

Mulberry Lane

Windsor Lane

Stonehill

East Stoke

Street

eet

Street

Leland    Trail

**I**

Mason Lane

Hyde
Lwr Rd

Hyde Road

Stanchester
Community School

Montacute    Road

Wash

**2**

17

Bishopston

Wash La

PH

Mido
St

Hedgecock La

Monarch's Way

St Michael's Hill

Hedgecock Hill

Monarch's Way

Monarch's Way

**3**

Park Vw

Townse

**32**

Lane

Road

Leland    Trail

✠ Ham Hill
Country Park

Hollow

**4**

Park    L

16

Liberty Trail

**5**

Liberty    Trail

Liberty    Trail

Liberty    Trail

**Little Norton**

Liberty

48

Westbury
Farm    49

**E**    **F**    **G**    **H**

Trail

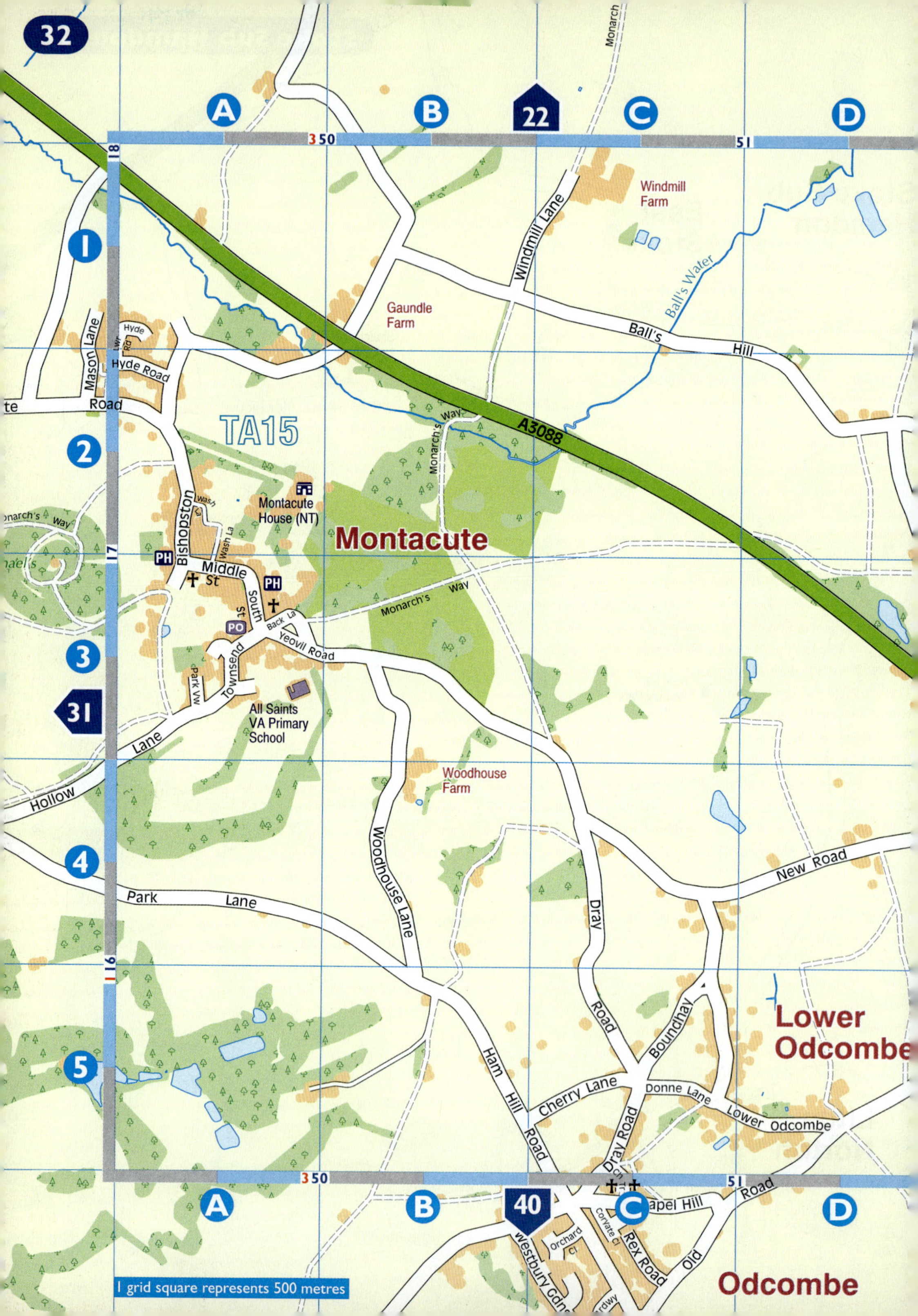

A · 350 · B · 22 · C · 51 · D

I
2
17
3
31
4
116
5

Monarch

Windmill Lane

Windmill Farm

Ball's Water

Gaundle Farm

Ball's    Hill

Mason Lane

Hyde
Hyde Rd
Hyde Road

Road

TA15

Monarch's Way

A3088

Monarch's Way

Montacute House (NT)

Bishopston

Wash La

Montacute

PH

Middle St

PH

South St

PO

Back La

Yeovil Road

Monarch's    Way

Park VW

Townsend Lane

All Saints VA Primary School

Woodhouse Farm

Hollow

Woodhouse Lane

Park    Lane

New Road

Dray Road

Boundhay

Lower Odcombe

Ham Hill Road

Cherry Lane

Donne Lane

Lower   Odcombe

Dray Road

A · 350 · B · 40 · C · 51 · D

westbury cnr

Orchard Ct

Corvate Cl

Rex Road

Chapel Hill

Old   Road

Odcombe

Tintinhull Road

E 52 F 23 G 53 H I

Larkhill

Thorne Coffin

Thorne Lane

Bethvil Road

Tintagel

King Arthur Drive

2

Shrewsbury Rd

Mereyale

Stnigh

Thorn Gdns

Poplar Dr

Merlin Rd

Percivale Rd

Tristan Cl

Ermine Rd

Stourton Way

Forde Pk

Forde Park

Copse Road

Boundary Way

Western Avenue

Yeovil Town FC

Preston CE Primary School

Acer Dr

3

Lufton College of FE

George Smith Wy

Mucheiney

Micheiney Wy

Westmister Wy

Flax Way

Hawkins Way

The Toose

Surg

Trading Est

Glastonbury

34

Armoury Rd

Limber Rd

Artillery Rd

Yeovil Small Business Cen

Memorial Rd

Grd Av

Mannesbury Wy

Richmond Rd

Priory Cl

Milton Cl

Derwent Way

White

Broadleaze

Lufton Trading Estate

Lufton

Clayton Close

Mrry Smith

M S D

George Smith

Warrior Av

Scimitar Av

Challenger Wy

Avenue

Houndstone

The Cleve

Sutton Gra

Tresco

Evesham Av

The Torre

Abbey Manor

Lufton

4

Roe Avenue

Bond St

Buckle Pl

Woodmeade

Houndstone Bus Park

Stourton

Tintern

Long

Preston Road

New Road

Ritchie Rd

Gunners La

Bigger Rd

Preston

Aling La

Jasmine Cl

Poppy Cl

Way

Road

Houndstone Retail Pk

Yeovil Crematorium

P

Works

Superstore

Higher Farm Trading Est

Preston Pluckne

High Leaze Farm

Fennel Way

Foxglove Way

Bluebell

Wisteria Cl

Alvington La

Lupin Wy

Alvington Lane

Bunford La

5

Alvington

Bunford Lane

Brympton Avenue

A3088

Bunford Lane

Watercombe Lane

Brympton D'Evercy

Brympton Hou

Council Building

Watercombe

A3088

Trading Estate

Merlin Road

Lufton

34

Tintinhull Road

A

Coppits Hill

ROAD

B

A37

24

Marshes Hill Farm

C

Lane

D

gg Farm

I

BA21

Garden Centre

Thorne La

Combe Street

Lane

Coombe St La

Thorne Lane

Combe

Winston Dr

Chilton Gv

Chilto

Lane

Wessex Road

Court Gdns

Court Gdns

Tintinhull Road

Marsh Lane

Park

Coniston Gdns

Thorne Lane

Thornton Rd

Thorne Thornton Rd

Greenwood Road

Boundary Cl

Alastair Dr

Combe Pk

Merevale Wy

Stnlgn

Frtns

Tintagel

King Arthur Drive

Albert

Brady

Coronation Avenue

Thtct Ct

A37

ILCHESTER

Combe Pk

Holland

Lane

Thrm Thrn Gdns

Percivale Rd

Larkspur Crs

Larkspur Cr

Eliotts Drive

Barnet

Thatcham Ct

Stiby Road

Yeovil Athletic Arena

2

Prston CE imary School

Pop La

Elmleigh

Acer Dr

Merlin Cl

Warling St

St Patrick's Rd

Springfield Rd

Marl Close

Marl Cl

Marl Cl

Thatcham Cl

PO

Newbury Terrace

Thatcham Pk

Tm Pk

Raglan Ter

Thatcham Close

Westfield Crs

Southway

Picket La

Yeovil College

The Toose

Derwent Way

Surg

Trading Est

Ermina St

Abbots Wy

Stiby Road

St Anne's Gdns

Frdm Av

Westfield Pl

Westfield Av

Westfield Grove

Southway

SC

2

3

Tresco Sch

Evesham Av

Beaulieu Dr

Monks

Abbey Rd

Freedom Avenue

Westfield Community School

Westfield Rd

Legion Rd

Oakridge Park Cemetery

Yeovil College

The torre

Malvern Bowleaze

Jurassic

Horton

Plover

Dale

Monks Dl

Burroughes Avenue

Cedar Grove

Westfield Infants Community Sch

Summerlands

Legion Rd

Grove

Willow Road

33

White Mead

Broadleaze

Preston School

Shrewsbury Rd

Home Drive

Ferndale Gdns

The Preston Hotel

Cncl Bldng

Preston Road

Abbey Manor

Long Mead

James's prkt

Meade

Abbots

Tisbury School

Cambridge Cl

Christopher Cl

Preston Road

Summerleaze Park

St Andrews Road

Parcroft Gdns

Grove Avenue

Yeovil College School of Art

West Park

Preston Road

The Park

Sydney Gdns

Swallowcliffe

Park School

KINGS

Yeo Squ

Surg

Supers

Superstore

Higher Farm Trading Est

Preston Road

Tithe

Century Park

Westbourne Grove

Westbourne Close

Parfields

Parcroft Junior Schools

Andrews Rd

Linden Rd

Preston Grove Medical Centre

Carlton Rd

Brooke Gdns

Sandown

Huish Gardens

Prim Sch

Park Gdns

Cncl Bldng

P

Health Centre

Preston Plucknett

Yeovil Aerodrome

Dodham Crs

Seaton

PO

Huish

West Street

Orchard Rd

Hallet Gdns

Richmond Rd

Cncl Bldng

Queensway A30

P

Hendford

Manor Rd

unford Lane

Works

Westland Road

Road

Beer Street

West Hendford

Police Station

BEDFORD HILL

Council Building

A

Watercombe Park

Merlin Road

Gazelle Cl

B

42

Works

C

Westfield Works

LYSANDER WAY A3088

Nursery Road

D

Somerset Place

P

Trading Estate

Lynx Trading Est

Superstore

Superstore

Woods

BA2

1 grid square represents 500 metres

E  F  25  G  Primrose Lane  H

56  Lyde Road  57

18

I

A359

Hundred Stone

ROAD

Fairmead Road
Fairmead Road
Fairmead Special School

Tower Road

St Mary's Crescent
Bucklers Mead Road
Runnymede Road

Constable Cl

Magna Close
Magna Cl

Cavalier

Gainsborough Way

Trent Cl
Crtn Cl

Redwood Road

Sandlewood Cl

High Lea
Lea Cl
High Lea

High
Cchrn
Bcknell

St Michael's Avenue
Bicknell Gdns

Bucklers Mead
Birchfield Road

Rivers Road

Cavalier Way

Bedford Rd
Hertford
Hertford Rd

Wilton Rd
Astw
Ashw Dr

Romsey Rd

Bucklers Mead Community School

Northbrook Road

St John's Rd
Birchfield Rd

Birchfield Primary School

Blenheim Rd

Pen Mill Trading Estate

Marksview Business Cen

Avenue
Elmhurst Av

The Hollies
Woodstock Rd

B Rd
Surgery

St John's Road

St John's Rd

2

Oxford Rd

Babylon Vw

Cheiston Avenue

Neathem Road

Milford Junior Sch

Milford Infants School

Wingate Av
Winchester Gdns

Heather Rd
Greenhill Rd

Monmouth Road

Netherton Road

Hawthorn Road

Meadow Road

Welbeck Road

Montrose Rd

Woburn Rd
Wentworth Rd
Marlborough Rd

Arundel Rd

Vale Road

Yeovil Business Centre

Lyde La

Grass Royal

Highfield Trading Est

Charles Road

Mayfield Rd

Hathermead Gdns

Mrbrgh Rd

Balmoral
Howard

Pen Mill

3

Pen Mill Trad Estate

36

Highfield Road

Cheiston Avenue

Melrose Road

Fielding Rd

Surg

St Michael's Avenue

Rosebery

Percy Road
Glenville

Alexandra Rd
Cromwell Rd

Victoria Rd
Sandringham

Fiveways School

Clifton

Buckland Road

Pen Mill Trading Estate Works

Goldcroft

Milford Road

Long Cl
Parreeve

King Street

Gordon Rd

Grass Royal

Grass Royal Junior School

Matthews Road

Pen Mill Infant School

Victoria Rd

Camborne St
Camborne Cv

3

4

KLEFORD

A30

Cattle Market

Kiddles Works

Reckleford Infant Sch

Eastville

Westville

Eastshill

Great Western Ter

Wyndham VW

Wyndham Hill

A30

SHERBORNE ROAD

Yeovil Pen Mill Station Works

Flushing Meadow

Compton Road

16

Fire Stn
Amb Stn
Bus Stn

Shop Cen

Yeovil Coll

Central Rd

P Works
Ivel Court

Penfield

Riverside Walk

Superstore

BABYLON HILL

5

Yeovil Golf Club

Golf Course

South

Penn House Day Hosp

Mill Lane Trading Estate

Newton Road

Yeo Leisure Park

Ski Centre

YEOVIL

Newton Surmaville

Leaze Lane

Swan Theatre

E  56  F  43  G  57  H

Summerhouse Hill

River Yeo

**A** **B** **26** **C** **D**

**1**

**2**

**3**

**35**

**4**

**5**

**A** **B** **44** **C** **D**

County

Trent Brook

18

3 58

59

Trent Cl

Redwood Rd

Sandlewood Cl

Wilton Rd

Ashw Dr

Romsey Rd

Ashwood Dr

Lyde Road

Lyde Road

Babylon W

117ord Road

Pen Mill Trading Estate

Marksview Business Cen

Oxford Rd

Lwthr Rd

Pmbrk Cl

Blvdr Rd

Arundel Rd

Howard Rd

Vale Road

Yeovil Business Centre

Lyde La

Pen Mill Trading Estate

Pen Mill

Buckl

g Estate

Ne Co

Over Comp

Western Street

Lwr Farm

Compton Acres

St Michaels Cl

Butterf House

Compton Road

Marl Lane

Compton Road

A30

ROAD

116

BABYLON HILL

Superstore

Meadow

Yeovil Golf Club

Leaze Lane

East Farm

Underdown Hollow

River Yeo

3 58

59

I grid square represents 500 metres

Mill

B3148

E F **27** G H

Monarch's Way

60 61 18

**I**

Crossfields

Folly La

Tucker's Cross

**2**

Crssfld

17

Plum Orch

Compton Road

Hart's La

Ratleigh Lane

Gooseland Lane

(Track)

**3**

**38**

**Stallen**

Ratleigh Lane

Ratleigh Lane

**4**

BABYLON HILL A30

LOW'S

Hill Lane

16

Halfway House

Noor Farm

**5**

Bedmill Farm

60 61

E F **45** G H

Silverlake Farm

B3148

Monarch's Way

A

362

B

28

C

Sandford Orcas Road

Macmillan Way

D

63

1

MARSTON

Hardings House Lane

ROAD

Trent Path Lane

2

Trent Path Lane

The Sheeplands

Highmore Rd

Nthrcmb Ln

Coombe

Works

Sheeplands Lane

**Sherborne**

17

Barton Gdns

Trent Path Lane

3

A30 YEOVIL ROAD

KITT

37

Works

Bradford Rd

Sherborne School for Girls

Acre Coo

The Sherborne Hotel

HORSECASTLES LANE

Richmond

Richmond Close

Richmond

Bradford Road

Horcastles La

Horcastles Crs

Horcastles

Wynnes Ri

Half Acres

4

Bradford

Gainsborough Drive

St Mary's Rd

St Catherine's St

St Catherine's Crs

Wscl

Sprng Fld

A352

PH

Midle La

St Mary's Rd

St Mary's Rd

Ridgeway

Wstrdg

OTTE

Abbots Way

Ridgeway

Ridgeway

South Noake

Works

Cemetery

16

Hill Lane

Wydford Cl

Askwith Cl

Littlefield

South Rd

Lenthay Road

Clarkfield

Westfield

Westfield

South Avenue

Lenthay Dairy House

5

Westbridge Park

Lee

Brow Hill

Hunts Mead

Lenthay

Honeycombe Rise

Silverlake Farm

A

362

B

Sherborne Abbey imary School

46

LC

C

63

Mill

Works

D

Lenthay Common

LC

I grid square represents 500 metres

E    F    **29**    G    H

64    65

The Gryphon School

St Aldhelm's Road

BRISTOL ROAD B3145

Castle Town Way

Coldharbour Business Park

Castle Town Way

McCreery Rd

St Pauls Green

St Paul's St

Granville Way

Coldharbour Hosp

Oliver Dr

Strdn

Carr Lane

Lane

Vernalis Road

Simons Rd

The Furlongs

Kings Ross

Sherborne Prim Sch

Harbour Rd

Harbour Way

Woolton Gr

Granville Way

Lambfield

Cl

Admrls

Cl

Earls Cl

Works

Business Park

Blackmarsh Farm

COLD HARBOUR

A30

CRACKMORE

A30

Kings Road

Grove Medical Cen

COLD HARBOUR

NORTH ROAD

The Avenue

Langdons

Chandlers

Dunstan

F.Mn.St.

School Rd

Tinneys Lane

Castle Road

Castle Town Way

OBORNE ROAD B3145

Ho Cl

**DT9**

GREENHILL

Newland

St SWITHIN'S ROAD

Nwland Gdn

St Swithins

Cl

The Wilderness

Hound Street

Knotts Paddk

B3145

Castleton Road

Pinford Lane

Pinford Lane

Sherborne Old Castle

CHEAP STREET

PO

Medical Centre

East Mill Lane

Sherborne Lake

Sherborne School

LONG STREET

Sherborne Abbey

Eastbury Hotel

Sherborne Mus

Works

Sherborne Castle

PH

M

Digby Road

SOUTH STREET

B3145

Police Stn

Ludbourne Rd

Pageant Dr

Superstore

PH

Durrant Cl

Trende St

Hf Mn St

Dlwds

GAS HS

LC

Works

New Road

Home Farm

Riverside Works

NEW ROAD

B3145

Station

Sherborne Station

Sherborne FC

Dancing Hill

The Kennels

A352

SHERB

Gainsborough Hill

E    F    **47**    G    H

64    65

1   2   3   4   5

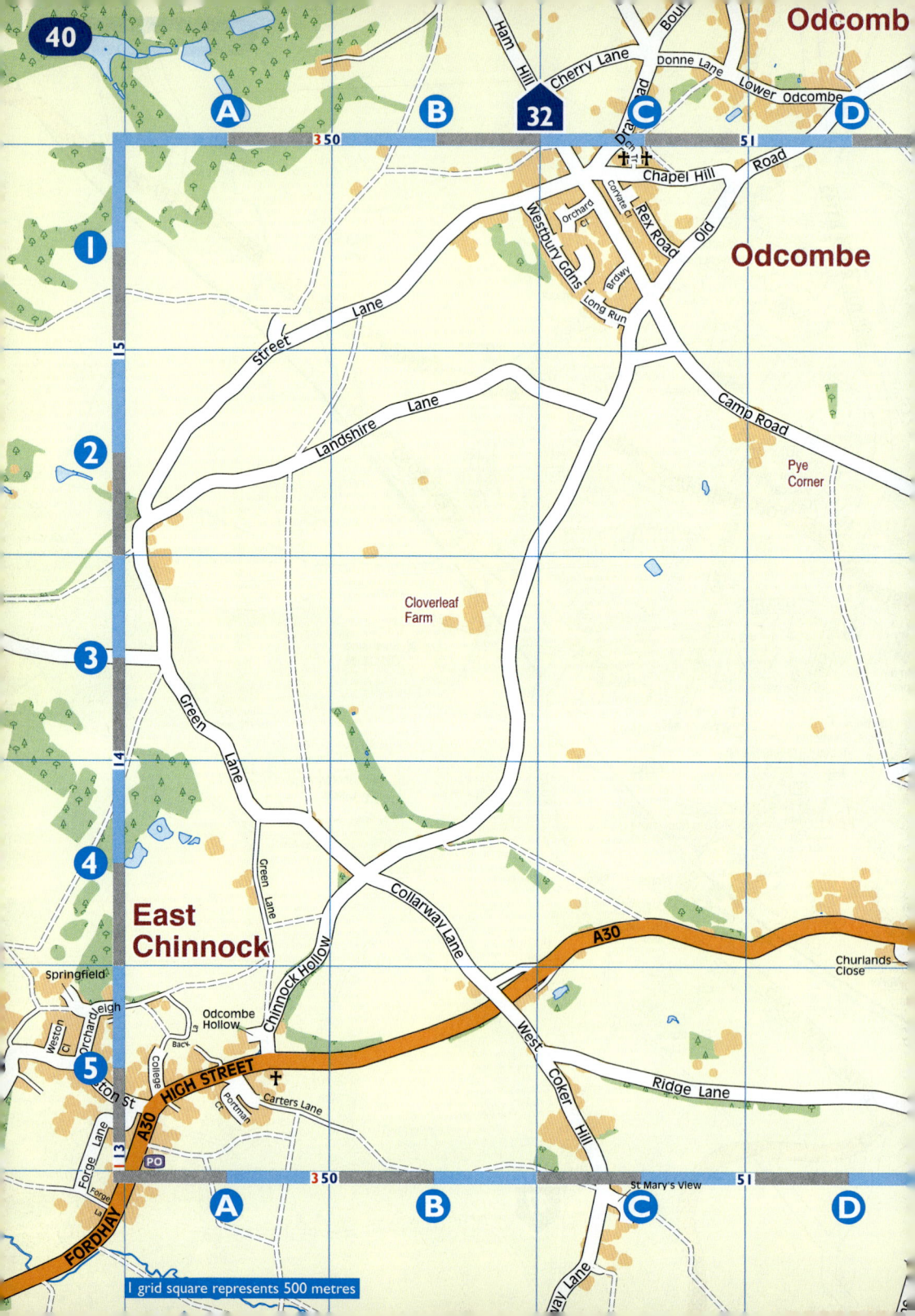

40

A  B  32  C  Odcomb  D

350          51

Cherry Lane
Donne Lane
Boul
Ham Hill
Lower Odcombe

Chapel Hill
Old Road

Odcombe

1

Westbury Gdns
Orchard Ct
Rex Road
Browy
Long Run
Street
Lane

Landshire Lane

Camp Road

2

Pye Corner

3

Green Lane

Cloverleaf Farm

14

4

Green Lane

Collarway Lane

East Chinnock

A30
Churlands Close

Springfield
Weston Cl
Orchard...leigh
Back
College
Odcombe Hollow
Chinnock Hollow

West Coker Hill
Ridge Lane

5

Eton St
HIGH STREET
Portman
Carters Lane

A30

113

Forge Lane
Forge La
PO

350          51

FORDHAY

A  B  St Mary's View  C  ...ay Lane  D

1 grid square represents 500 metres

E  F  33  G  H

52  53

Bunford Lane

Brympton House

Brympton D'Evercy

Council Building

Trading Estate

A3088

Brympton Way

Watercombe Way

Watercombe Road

Tradi

I

A3088  LYSA

Broadleaze Farm

Laburnum Way

Oakleigh

Birchdale  Ridgemead

Ashmead

The Spinne

2

St Mths Cl

Watercombe Hts

Coppice Cl

Rye  Gdns

Nathan

Camp Hill

Camp Road

WEST COKER RD

Helena Rd

Feebarrow

The Yeovil Court Hotel

Wyvern Close

Priory Cl

3

Nash

Pla
La

42

West Coker

A30

Green Lane

4

Manor Farm

Lane

Surg

Burton La

Burto

Lanes Hotel

Cedar Flds

Church St

HIGH STREET

Manor st

Dens'n

Manor Dr

Brdcrs

Broadacres

Hgr Burton

Wy

Long

Meadow Vw

Burton

Furlong

PO

East

Orchard Close

Laurel

Ryefields

Cl

Works

Burto

Ruddock

Ruddock Wy

Chestfields

Mill Lane

Mill Lane

5

PO

Mill Close

Font Villas

Lakefields

Halves Lane

Holywell

Font

Lane

Mill

Ea
Pr

52  53s

E  F  G  H

Halves Lane

Drks Mdw

Ridge

Yeovil Aerodrome

Flashn...

A B 34 C D

Bunford Lane

Works

Westland Road Road

Beer Street

Richi

WAY A30 Splt

The Crs

W Hendfo

W Manor Rd

Encl Bldg

Police Sta

Health Centre

354 rks

55 Y B

West Hendford

Millbrook

Westland Works

LYSANDER WAY A3088

P

Somerset Place

Council Building

Watercombe Park

Gazelle Road

Lynx Trading Est

Superstore

2

Nursery Road

Tr Est

1

Merlin Road

Trading Estate

Garrett Road

Superstore

Superstore

HENDFORD HILL

Southwoods

Dore Roa

BA2

Watercombe Lane

Sea King Rd

A3088 LYSANDER ROAD

Holly Trinity CE Primary School

Holly Tree Walk

Chestnut Av

Pine Tree Dr

Maple Dr

Rowan Way

Juniper

A30

A3088 WA

Ashmead

Laburnum Way

Wdct

Plantagenet

Lime Tree Avenue

Alder Cv

Old Barn Way

Forest Hill

Ivy Walk

Beechwood

Sycamore Dr

Oakleigh

Birchdale

Ridgemead

Russet Wy

Cypress Dr

Chase

Night Cls

Yew Tree Cl

Yew Tree Cl

forest hill

The Spinney

Cherry Tree

Coppice Cl

St Mrrns Wy

Watercombe Hts

Rye Gdns

Nathan Cl

WEST COKER ROAD

PO

Danielsfield Rd

Turner's Gdns

Arnewood Gdns

Barn Lane

Hillgrove Av

Windermere Cl

A30

Ltl Tarrat La

Tarratt Road

East Coker Road

2

Beaconfield Road

Wraxhill Road

Sandhurst Road

Lower Turners Barn La

Monarch's Way Tarratt Lane

DORCHESTER ROAD

Yeov Show

WEST COKER RD

Placket Lane

Bc Rd

Lower Wraxhill Rd

Yeovil Rd

Lower East Coker Rd

Keyford

Helena Road

Priory Cl

Placket Lane

Wroll Rd

3

The Yeovil Court Hotel

Nash Lane

Lane

41

14

4

Burton La

Longlands Lane

Gunville Lane

Pavyotts Lane

Monarch's Way

Pavyotts

Lane

Nash

Brdcrs

Broadacres

Hgr Burton Vw

Meadow Vw

Burton

Redlands

Monarch's Way

Furlong

Lane

PO

Mill Close

Tellis Cross

North Coker

Pavyotts Farm

5

Chantry View

Monarch's Way

113

354

55

Mill

East Coker Primary School

A B C D

Halves Lane

Drks M

Works

East

I grid square represents 500 metres

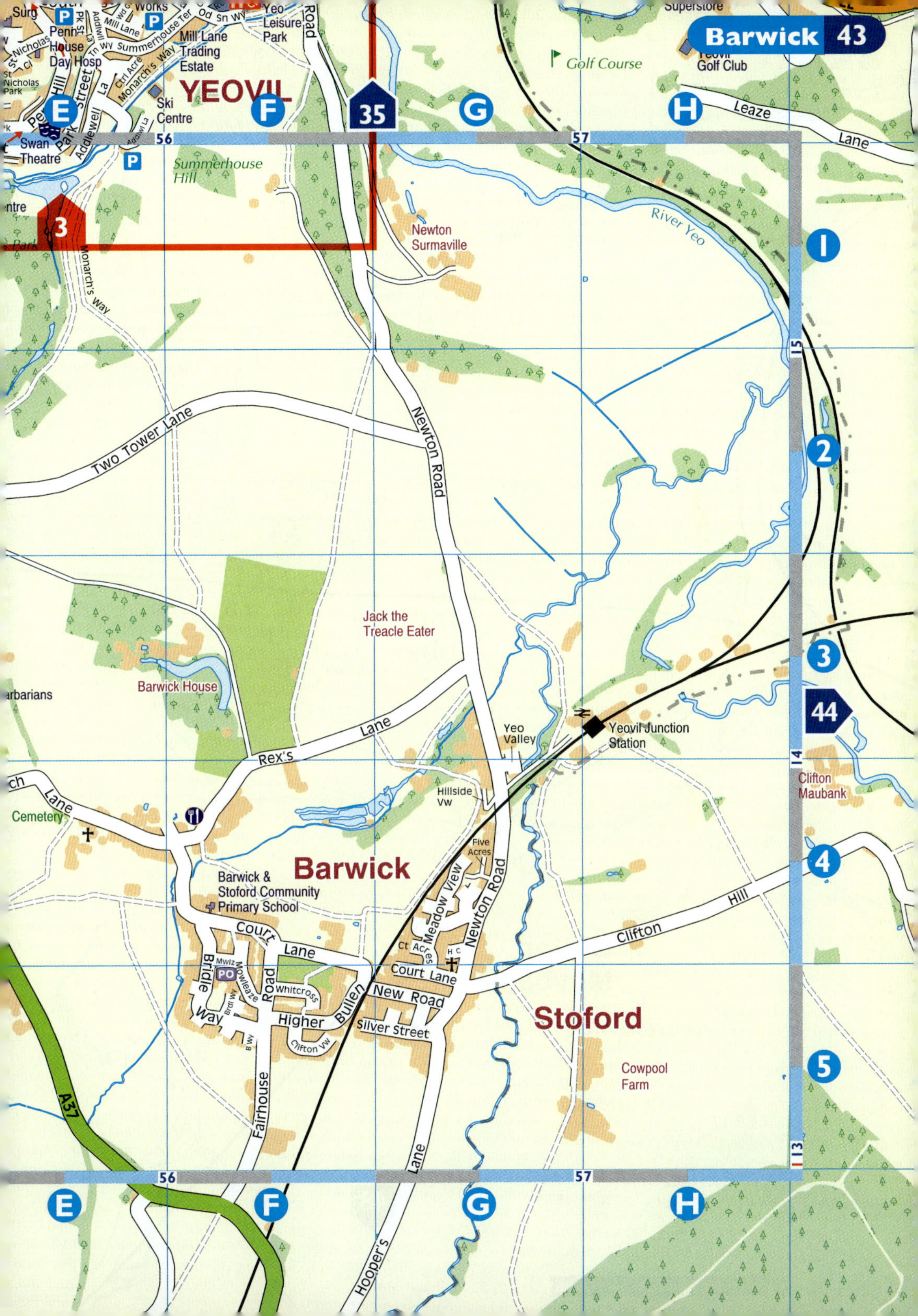

YEOVIL

Barwick

Stoford

River Yeo

Golf Course

Yeovil Golf Club

Leaze Lane

Superstore

Summerhouse Hill

Newton Surmaville

Two Tower Lane

Newton Road

Jack the Treacle Eater

Barwick House

Rex's Lane

Barbarians

Cemetery

Yeo Valley

Yeovil Junction Station

Clifton Maubank

Hillside Vw

Five Acres

Barwick & Stoford Community Primary School

Court Lane

Meadow View

Newton Road

Clifton Hill

Clifton

Bridle Way

Higher Road

Whitcross

Clifton Vw

Court Lane

New Road

Silver Street

Fairhouse

Hooper's Lane

Cowpool Farm

Mill Lane Trading Estate

Yeo Leisure Park

Penn House Day Hosp

Ski Centre

Swan Theatre

Monarch's Way

Summerhouse Ter

Works

St Nicholas Park

Hill Street

Park

Addlewell

35

44

A37

56    57

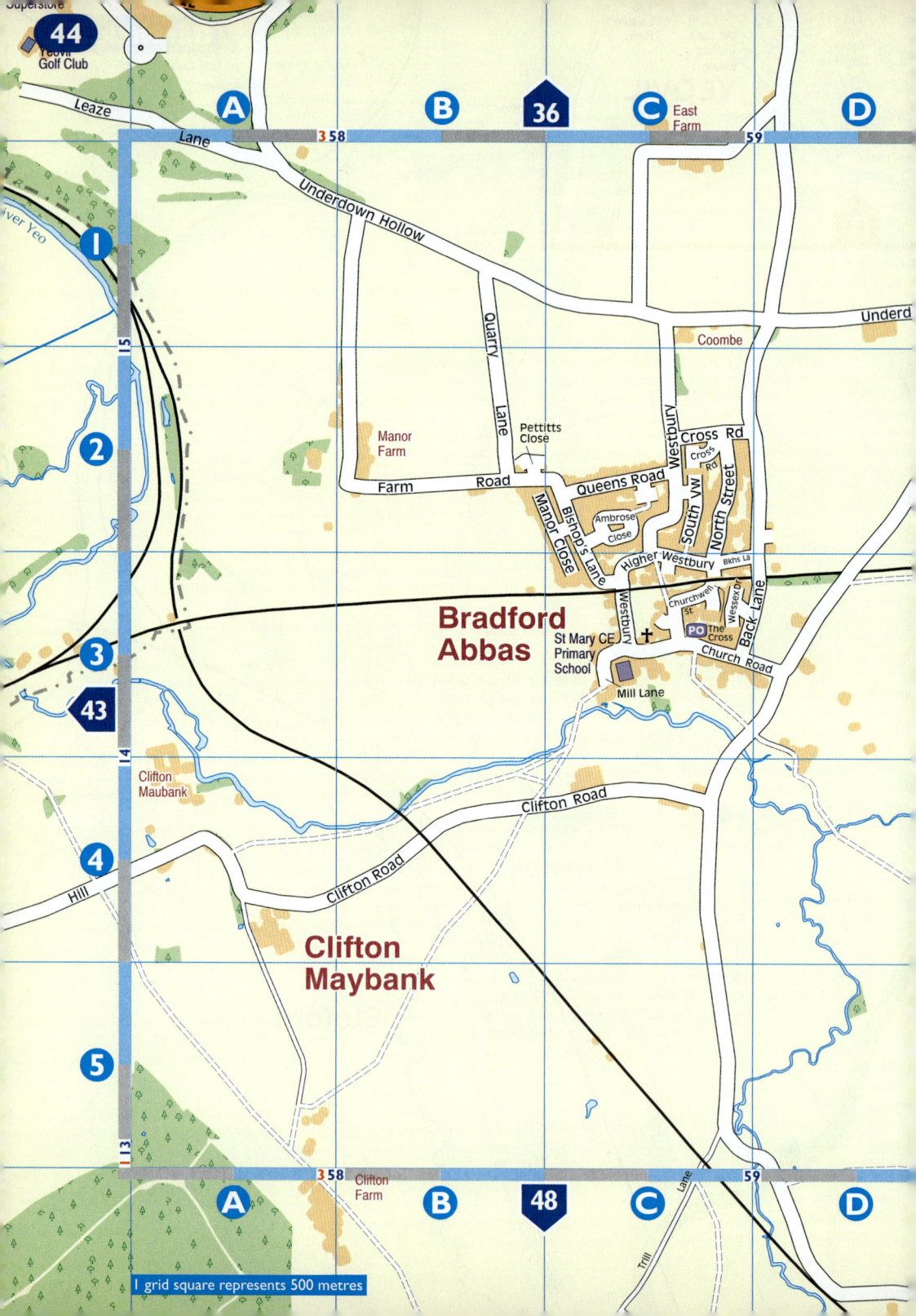

Superstore

**44** Yeovil Golf Club

Leaze Lane

3 58                                                        59

River Yeo

**1**

15

Underdown Hollow

Coombe

Underd

Quarry Lane

**2**

Manor Farm

Pettitts Close

Westbury     Cross Rd

Cross Rd

Farm          Road          Queens Road

Manor Close

South Vw     North Street

Bishop's Lane

Ambrose Close

Higher Westbury     Bkhs La

**3**

**43**

14

Westbury

Churchwell St     Wessex Dr     Back Lane

**Bradford Abbas**

St Mary CE Primary School

PO     The Cross

Church Road

Mill Lane

Clifton Maubank

Clifton Road

**4**

Hill

Clifton Road

**Clifton Maybank**

**5**

13

3 58     Clifton Farm                                       59

Lane

Trill

1 grid square represents 500 metres

E    F    37    G    H

60      61

Bedmill Farm

Silverlake Farm

**I**

15

**2**

Wyke Farm

River Yeo

River Ye

**3**

46

14

Lake Farm

**4**

Works

Sarum

The Paddocks

Eastfield

Eastfield

The Drove

Grange Park

Bembury Lane

The Waldrons

The Waldrons

Waldrons

Blackbirds

**Thornford**

Morston

Church Rd

Boot La

Glebe Cl

Thornford CE Prim Sch

Blacksmith's Lane

Pound

**5**

13

PO

E    F    49    G    H

60      61

Upton Rd

Ry Crs

ford Road

**A** 3 62 **B** **38** **C** 63 **D**

Lenthay
Dairy House

Hunts Mead

dge Park

Lenthay

Honeycombe

Silverlake
Farm

Sherborne Abbey
CE Primary School

Works

West

Mill

**I**

*Lenthay
Common*

LC

15

Honeycombe
Farm

Pound

**2**

Honeycombe
Wood

Court
House Dairy

Road

**3**

Pound

**45**

14

Lake Farm

**4**

KS

Higher
Farm

Street

Gordon's

**5**

Higher

Lane

13

**Lillington**

**A** 3 62 **B** **C** 63 **D**

Lower Street

B3145 NEW
A352
Sherborne
FC
Dancing Hill
The Kennels

**E** 64 **F** Gainsborough Hill **39** **G** 65 **H**

**I** 15

SHERBORNE HILL

A352

A3030

**2** West Lane

Nort
Woo

Westhill
Lodge

Macmillan Way

**3** A303

**4** 14

P

Leweston
Farm

Folke Lar

**5**

F

Broke Lane

Newcross
Kings Cl
Kings Cl
Orchard Cl
Dene Cl
Quarry Lane
**Longburton**

3

**E** 64 **F** **G** 65 **H** West Hall
A352
Spring
Ch Cl

**48**

A    B    **44**    C    D

3 58    59

Clifton
Farm

**1**

Clifton
Wood

Trill

Lane

Trill

Lane

Thornford
Station

**2**

Trill
Farm

13

12

**3**

**4**

Thornford

Road

St Andrews
CE Primary Schoo

Coles La

Curly-Clovermead

stonyacres

Clvrmd

Uplands

Bucklers
Mead

**5**

Down's    Lane

Church
Farm

**Ryme
Intrinseca**

Ryme    Road

High

High St

Queen St

St Osmund Cl

Melbury Road

Birch L

Tark's Hill

Common    Lane

Lane

Oakgate

A    3 58    B    C    59    D

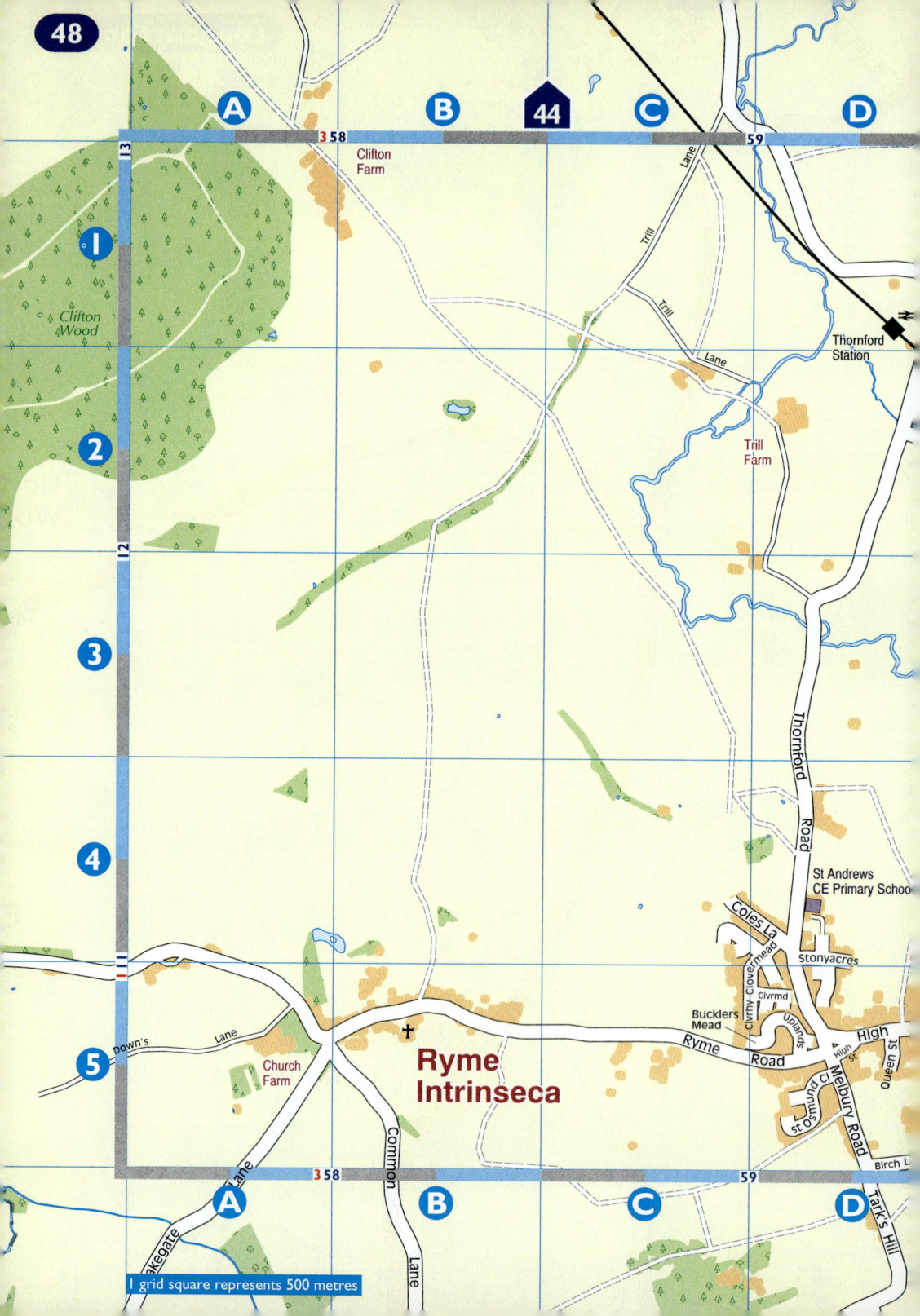

1 grid square represents 500 metres

Morston

Thornford
CE Prim Sch
Blacksmith's
Lane

Church Rd

Boot La

PO

45

E F G H

I

2

Beer
Hackett

Church Cl

Claypits Lane

3

Macmillan Way

Knighton

4

Whitfield
Farm

5

Yetminster
Station

The
Sidings
Works

Sussex
Farm Wy

Macmillan Way

Brierley Hay

Eastlands

Willow
Farm

aster

Brister

Downs La

Shearstones

Whitfield
Woods

E F G H

A 3 43 B 44 C D

I

Marks
Barn

Fords
Crofts Farm

Broadshard Rd

Ashlands
Meadow

Works

2

*Mancombe*

Hinton Road

North Street
Trading Estate

Ashland
Court

NORTH STREET

A356

Brick Yard La

Bincombe Drive

Windmill
Rd

Ashlands
CE First Sch

Works

Bincombe

Pople's Well

Rose Lane

School

Abbey St

Market
Square

PO

EAST STR

3

HARD

RD

A30 CHARD ROAD

Tuncombe Lane

**Roundham**

WEST STREET A30

Church Pth

CHURCH

ST

MARKET ST

The George
Shopping Cen

Indu
Esta

A35

Bulls
Lane

Lyewater

Bird's Cl

Works

Pulmans

Henhay

Barn Street

Middle Path

Bowhayes

Orchard Rise

4

Cathole Bridge Road

Hewish Lane

*Curriott
Hill*

Crewkerne
Hosp

Health
Cen

Barn Close

Barn Close

Currlott Hill Road

HERMITAGE STREET B3165

Priory Sq

Ivelway

Furland Road

Memorial Av

Rhyc

So

severalls park

severalls Rd

Langmead Road

Park View

Par

PO

Kith

5

Catholi Bridge Road

Curriott Hill

Fairfield

Hardy
Ct

Langmead Sq

Valley Rd

Vale
Cl

Cowen

B3165 LYME ROAD

Maiden Beech
Community
Middle School

Bushfield Road

Bushfield Road

Kingswood Rd

The Hollies

Manor Vw

Henley VW

Cathole 44 Bridge Road

LC

A 3 43 B Folly
Farm C D

**Hewish**

Hewish

A30

Liberty

Lower
Severalls Farm

adshard

Haselbu
Pluckne

M

**I**

Swan H

New

New Cl

YEOVIL    ROAD

A30

Holly
Grove

Oak Dr

Willow

Chesnut Av

el VW

Oak Dr

shlands

Sycmr
Dr

Road

Fox Meadows

H C

Wadham
School

Cemetery

Higher Easthams Lane

Lower
Easthams Farm

River Parrett Trail & Monarch's Way

**2**

10

Willis's

**3**

Pe
Hil

r Hl La

OUNT PLEASANT

asthams Rd

Butts    Quarry    Lane

**TA18**

River Parrett

**KERNE**

Cropmead
Trading Estate

Works

Blacknell Lane

Industrial
Estate

s

Blacknell
Industrial Estate

**4**

60

STREET

Drive

Kithill

Shute
Lake

Chariton Cl

La

Weavers Cl

Mill La

Winyards
Vw

Winyards Vw

Winyards
Vw

A356

STATION

Hellings
Farm

**5**

Lane

Mill

Bradford Rd

ROAD

Crewkerne
Station

LC

Works

A3066

Broughtons Dr

Clark's
Lane

Unity La

Newbery
Lane

Silver

Works

Packers W

Cathole Bridge Road

MIDDLE STR

La

## USING THE STREET INDEX

Street names are listed alphabetically. Each street name is followed by its postal town or area locality, the Postcode District, the page number, and the reference to the square in which the name is found.

Standard index entries are shown as follows:

**Abbey Cl** *SHER* DT9 ..................... **39** E4

Street names and selected addresses not shown on the map due to scale restrictions are shown in the index with an asterisk:

**Alder Gv** *CREWK* TA18 * ................. **50** D2

## GENERAL ABBREVIATIONS

| | | | |
|---|---|---|---|
| ACC ... ACCESS | E ... EAST | LDG ... LODGE | R ... R |
| ALY ... ALLEY | EMB ... EMBANKMENT | LGT ... LIGHT | RBT ... ROUNDAB |
| AP ... APPROACH | EMBY ... EMBASSY | LK ... LOCK | RD ... R |
| AR ... ARCADE | ESP ... ESPLANADE | LKS ... LAKES | RDG ... R |
| ASS ... ASSOCIATION | EST ... ESTATE | LNDG ... LANDING | REP ... REPU |
| AV ... AVENUE | EX ... EXCHANGE | LTL ... LITTLE | RES ... RESER |
| BCH ... BEACH | EXPY ... EXPRESSWAY | LWR ... LOWER | RFC ... RUGBY FOOTBALL C |
| BLDS ... BUILDINGS | EXT ... EXTENSION | MAG ... MAGISTRATES' | RI ... |
| BND ... BEND | F/O ... FLYOVER | MAN ... MANSIONS | RP ... |
| BNK ... BANK | FC ... FOOTBALL CLUB | MD ... MEAD | RW ... |
| BR ... BRIDGE | FK ... FORK | MDW ... MEADOWS | S ... SO |
| BRK ... BROOK | FLD ... FIELD | MEM ... MEMORIAL | SCH ... SCH |
| BTM ... BOTTOM | FLDS ... FIELDS | MI ... MILL | SE ... SOUTH |
| BUS ... BUSINESS | FLS ... FALLS | MKT ... MARKET | SER ... SERVICE |
| BVD ... BOULEVARD | FM ... FARM | MKTS ... MARKETS | SH ... S |
| BY ... BYPASS | FT ... FORT | ML ... MALL | SHOP ... SHOP |
| CATH ... CATHEDRAL | FTS ... FLATS | MNR ... MANOR | SKWY ... SKY |
| CEM ... CEMETERY | FWY ... FREEWAY | MS ... MEWS | SMT ... SU |
| CEN ... CENTRE | FY ... FERRY | MSN ... MISSION | SOC ... SOC |
| CFT ... CROFT | GA ... GATE | MT ... MOUNT | SP ... |
| CH ... CHURCH | GAL ... GALLERY | MTN ... MOUNTAIN | SPR ... SP |
| CHA ... CHASE | GDN ... GARDEN | MTS ... MOUNTAINS | SQ ... SQ |
| CHYD ... CHURCHYARD | GDNS ... GARDENS | MUS ... MUSEUM | ST ... ST |
| CIR ... CIRCLE | GLD ... GLADE | MWY ... MOTORWAY | STN ... STA |
| CIRC ... CIRCUS | GLN ... GLEN | N ... NORTH | STR ... STR |
| CL ... CLOSE | GN ... GREEN | NE ... NORTH EAST | STRD ... STR |
| CLFS ... CLIFFS | GND ... GROUND | NW ... NORTH WEST | SW ... SOUTH |
| CMP ... CAMP | GRA ... GRANGE | O/P ... OVERPASS | TDG ... TRA |
| CNR ... CORNER | GRG ... GARAGE | OFF ... OFFICE | TER ... TER |
| CO ... COUNTY | GT ... GREAT | ORCH ... ORCHARD | THWY ... THROUGH |
| COLL ... COLLEGE | GTWY ... GATEWAY | OV ... OVAL | TNL ... TU |
| COM ... COMMON | GV ... GROVE | PAL ... PALACE | TOLL ... TOL |
| COMM ... COMMISSION | HGR ... HIGHER | PAS ... PASSAGE | TPK ... TURN |
| CON ... CONVENT | HL ... HILL | PAV ... PAVILION | TR ... T |
| COT ... COTTAGE | HLS ... HILLS | PDE ... PARADE | TRL ... |
| COTS ... COTTAGES | HO ... HOUSE | PH ... PUBLIC HOUSE | TWR ... TO |
| CP ... CAPE | HOL ... HOLLOW | PK ... PARK | U/P ... UNDER |
| CPS ... COPSE | HOSP ... HOSPITAL | PKWY ... PARKWAY | UNI ... UNIVE |
| CR ... CREEK | HRB ... HARBOUR | PL ... PLACE | UPR ... |
| CREM ... CREMATORIUM | HTH ... HEATH | PLN ... PLAIN | V ... |
| CRS ... CRESCENT | HTS ... HEIGHTS | PLNS ... PLAINS | VA ... VA |
| CSWY ... CAUSEWAY | HVN ... HAVEN | PLZ ... PLAZA | VIAD ... VIA |
| CT ... COURT | HWY ... HIGHWAY | POL ... POLICE STATION | VIL ... |
| CTRL ... CENTRAL | IMP ... IMPERIAL | PR ... PRINCE | VIS ... |
| CTS ... COURTS | IN ... INLET | PREC ... PRECINCT | VLG ... VIL |
| CTYD ... COURTYARD | IND EST ... INDUSTRIAL ESTATE | PREP ... PREPARATORY | VLS ... |
| CUTT ... CUTTINGS | INF ... INFIRMARY | PRIM ... PRIMARY | VW ... |
| CV ... COVE | INFO ... INFORMATION | PROM ... PROMENADE | W ... |
| CYN ... CANYON | INT ... INTERCHANGE | PRS ... PRINCESS | WD ... W |
| DEPT ... DEPARTMENT | IS ... ISLAND | PRT ... PORT | WHF ... W |
| DL ... DALE | JCT ... JUNCTION | PT ... POINT | WK ... |
| DM ... DAM | JTY ... JETTY | PTH ... PATH | WKS ... |
| DR ... DRIVE | KG ... KING | PZ ... PIAZZA | WLS ... |
| DRO ... DROVE | KNL ... KNOLL | QD ... QUADRANT | WY ... |
| DRY ... DRIVEWAY | L ... LAKE | QU ... QUEEN | YD ... |
| DWGS ... DWELLINGS | LA ... LANE | QY ... QUAY | YHA ... YOUTH HO |

# OSTCODE TOWNS AND AREA ABBREVIATIONS

## Index - streets

## Abb - Cro

## U

## V

## W

## Y

## Index - featured places

## Acknowledgements

ols address data provided by Education Direct.

station information supplied by Johnsons.

n centre information provided by:

n Centre Association ⚙ Britains best garden centres

le Garden Centres 💐

atement on the front cover of this atlas is sourced, selected and quoted
reader comment and feedback form received in 2004

**How do I find the perfect place?**

# **AA** **Street by Street** QUESTIONNAIRE

**Dear Atlas User**
**Your comments, opinions and recommendations are very important to us.**
**So please help us to improve our street atlases by taking a few minutes**
**to complete this simple questionnaire.**

You do not need a stamp (unless posted outside the UK). If you do not want to remove this page from your street atlas, then photocopy it or write your answers on a plain sheet of paper.

**Send to: Marketing Assistant, AA Publishing, 14th Floor Fanum House,**
**Freepost SCE 4598, Basingstoke RG21 4GY**

## ABOUT THE ATLAS...

**Please state which city / town / county you bought:**

_____

**Where did you buy the atlas?** (City, Town, County)

_____

**For what purpose?** (please tick all applicable)

**To use in your local area** ☐   **To use on business or at work** ☐

**Visiting a strange place** ☐   **In the car** ☐   **On foot** ☐

**Other** (please state)

_____

**Have you ever used any street atlases other than AA Street by Street?**

Yes ☐   No ☐

**If so, which ones?**

_____

**Is there any aspect of our street atlases that could be improved?**
(Please continue on a separate sheet if necessary)

_____
_____
_____

ML139z

continued overleaf

**Please list the features you found most useful:**

_____
_____
_____

**Please list the features you found least useful:**

_____
_____
_____
_____

## LOCAL KNOWLEDGE...

Local knowledge is invaluable. Whilst every attempt has been made to make the information contained in this atlas as accurate as possible, should you notice any inaccuracies, please detail them below (if necessary, use a blank piece of paper) or e-mail us at *streetbystreet@theAA.com*

_____
_____
_____
_____

## ABOUT YOU...

**Name (Mr/Mrs/Ms)** _____

**Address** _____

**Postcode** _____

**Daytime tel no** _____

**E-mail address** _____


**Which age group are you in?**

Under 25 ☐    25-34 ☐    35-44 ☐    45-54 ☐    55-64 ☐    65+ ☐

Are you an AA member?    YES ☐    NO ☐

Do you have Internet access?    YES ☐    NO ☐

_____

Thank you for taking the time to complete this questionnaire. Please send it to us as soon as possible, and remember, you do not need a stamp (unless posted outside the UK).

We may use information we hold about you to, telephone or email you about other products and services offered by the AA, we do NOT disclose this information to third parties.

Please tick here if you do not wish to hear about products and services from the AA. ☐

ML139z